Celebrate!

STORIES OF THE JEWISH HOLIDAYS

Celeb

STORIES OF THE

BY GILDA BERGER

SCHOLASTIC INC.
New York Toronto London Auckland Sydney
Mexico City New Delhi Hong Kong

rate!

JEWISH HOLIDAYS

PAINTINGS BY **PETER CATALANOTTO**

ACKNOWLEDGMENTS

I thank my wonderful daughters, Ellie and Nancy, for encouraging me to write this book; my dear friend, Dan Groden, for consulting with me on Judaism; Rabbi Melinda Panken and Rabbi Joel Sisenwine for their careful reading of the manuscript; Tracy Mack and Jean Feiwel of Scholastic Press for their unstinting devotion to this project; and my husband, Mel, for forty joyous years of holiday celebrations.

ISBN 0-590-93708-1

12 11 10 9 8 7 6 5 4 3 2 1   9/9 0 1 2 3 4/0

Printed in the U.S.A.   14

First Scholastic Book Club printing, November 1999

The illustrations in this book were painted in watercolor. The display type was set in Linoscript, Copperplate 33bc, and Mantinia. The text type was set in 13 pt. Galliard. Book design by Marijka Kostiw.

Contents

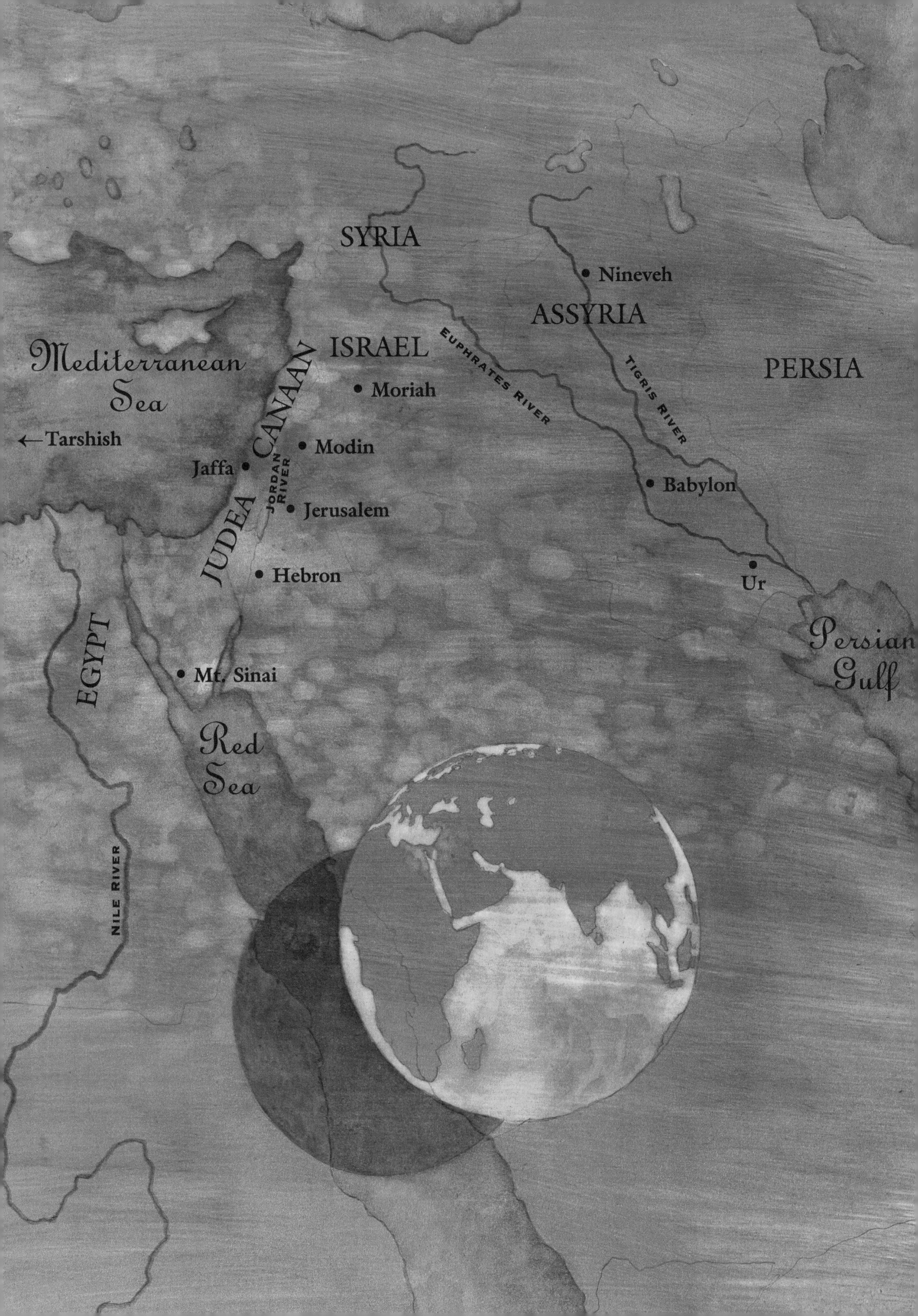
SYRIA
Nineveh
ASSYRIA
ISRAEL
CANAAN
Mediterranean Sea
EUPHRATES RIVER
TIGRIS RIVER
PERSIA
Moriah
← Tarshish
Modin
Jaffa
JORDAN RIVER
Jerusalem
Babylon
JUDEA
Hebron
Ur
EGYPT
Persian Gulf
Mt. Sinai
Red Sea
NILE RIVER

Introduction

MY FAMILY WELCOMES every reason to celebrate. We celebrate birthdays for several days — and we take the same joy in celebrating the Jewish holidays as we do in having birthday parties! As book people — as well as "People of the Book" — every holiday celebration involves getting the right book to fit the occasion.

With four curious and active grandchildren, I had developed a little ritual that everyone seemed to like. Just before we sat down to a festive holiday meal, we gathered together to share a book that captured the mood and spirit of the particular holiday. Sometimes we had to settle for a book that had great pictures but too difficult a text. Other times, we read a folktale that everyone loved, but that told little about the how and the why of the celebration. Also, few of the books I used put the holidays into a historical context or suggested ways of extending the observance with cooking or other activities.

Gradually I began to realize that what was needed was a retelling of the stories that come to mind when we think *Jewish holiday*. What is Hanukkah without the story of Judah and the Maccabees? What is Purim without the story of Esther and Mordecai?

I wanted to write a book that retold these best-known stories for children. The book would be one that was suitable for children of all ages, and one that could be easily read aloud by youngsters or to young children by their parents or grandparents. In retelling the stories, I hoped to bring out the meaning and, most of all, the spirit of the holiday.

Wouldn't it be fun, I thought, if the book also had activities and recipes for each holiday? After all, what is a celebration without the games and the preparation and sweet anticipation of the holiday meals?

Out of my attempts to make my own family holiday celebrations more joyous came *Celebrate! Stories of the Jewish Holidays.* It is my hope that it can make your celebrations especially wonderful, and will be just the book you will want to read and share with your own family as the holidays come around, each in its own season.

GILDA BERGER
EAST HAMPTON, NEW YORK
SEPTEMBER 25, 1997

About the Book

THE JEWISH HOLIDAYS ARE OFTEN CALLED the jewels in the crown of the Jewish year. Each holiday marks a major event in the history of the Jewish people: a miraculous happening, a valiant search for freedom, or a desperate struggle for survival. Each holiday also celebrates a particular season of the year and the natural cycle of time. Thus, the historical holidays of Purim, Pesach, and Shavuot are also the holidays of spring. Sukkot, which marks the wandering in the desert after the Exodus from Egypt, is also the time of the harvest, before the coming of winter.

The holidays come at the same season each year, but every holiday came into being at a different time in history. Pesach, which recalls the freeing of the Jews from Egyptian slavery, dates back more than one thousand years before the first Hanukkah. Esther, the heroine of the story of Purim, is believed to have lived some fourteen hundred years after the time of Abraham, father of the Jews, whom we read about at Rosh Hashanah. Taken together, the holidays are part of a tradition that is over three thousand years old.

Over the course of history, the Jewish people scattered and came to live all over the world. The customs, traditions, and even language differed from place to place. Jews who settled in central and eastern Europe spoke a language called Yiddish, which is based on German, with a little Hebrew, French, Polish, and Russian mixed in. People whose families came from these Yiddish-speaking Jews are called

Ashkenazim. Jews who originally settled in Spain or Portugal developed a language, called Ladino, that was mostly Spanish, Hebrew, and Arabic. Descendants from Ladino or Arabic-speaking Jews are called *Sephardim.*

The ceremonies and rituals of each holiday went through many changes, too. But the Bible often speaks of Jews as *B'nai Yisrael,* the "Children of Israel." This tells us that no matter where Jews live, they're like a family. And like any family, they have similar experiences, a shared history, and a kindred spirit that unites them. So even though the Children of Israel may be spread all over the world, the spirit of the holidays they celebrate is the same everywhere.

Through the ages, storytellers in each generation have told and retold the same holiday tales from Jewish history and legend. Many of the favorites are in this book. All of the stories come from the Bible, except for the Hanukkah story, "Miracle of Lights," which comes from another sacred text called the Apocrypha.

The stories and holidays help bind the Jewish family together. They strengthen and deepen their unity and purpose. They keep alive their memories and way of life. They put them in tune with nature and the changing seasons. They give the Jewish people ideas about how to live their lives. They make them think about the kind of people they are and the kind of people they would like to be.

The stories are meant to be a springboard to learning more about Jewish traditions. They are also meant to inspire the reader to ask questions and to find his or her own meanings in the spirit of the Jewish holidays.

Celebrate!

STORIES OF THE JEWISH HOLIDAYS

Shabbat

CREATION OF THE WORLD

"SIX DAYS SHALL WORK BE DONE, BUT THE SEVENTH DAY
IS A SABBATH OF SOLEMN REST."

Leviticus 23:3

ONCE THERE WAS NOTHING AT ALL on Earth but water. It was the very beginning of time, the dawn of history. The world was formless and empty. No living things. No plants or trees. Only the Spirit of God moving over a dark and endless stretch of water.

God looked out over the boundless black waters. All was bleak and dull and dreary. The waters were colorless and without life.

"Let there be light!" God said. And suddenly there was light everywhere.

The waters gleamed and glistened. The brightness scattered the darkness. The light revealed a mysterious, hidden world. God saw that it was good.

But the dazzling brightness was also overpowering. It seemed constant and never ending. So God, the Great Creator, separated light from darkness, in order to have some of each. "I will call Light, Day. And I will call Darkness, Night," said God. And so it was. It was the very first day.

The next morning, God looked at the limitless water in the world. "There is too much of it," said God.

So the Great Creator cut it in half. "One half will be raised. It will become a splendid roof over the water below," said God.

Suddenly the sky filled with mists and clouds. There were light rays of every color. God looked up and saw the arch that the colors formed in the sky.

"I will call the roof of the world Heaven," said God. And so it was, the second day of the creation of the world.

The following morning God gazed over the big stretches of unbroken water. Something was missing. God said, "Let the waters under Heaven be gathered together in one place, and let the dry land appear."

And so it was. God swept over the water, and on it drew different shapes. Where God moved, there appeared dry land. The land became separated from the water. "All the pieces of land," said God, "will be called Earth. And all the water will be called the Seas."

But the shapes of Earth looked bare. So God covered the barrenness with trees and plants.

"Let every kind contain its own seed," said God. "Thus, each will have offspring, and continue to reproduce." And so it was. It was the third day.

Then God created the heavenly bodies. Outside the Earth, God placed two globes of light. The larger one, God called Sun. It was to look after the Day. The smaller one, God called Moon. It was for the Night.

At the same time, God made millions of smaller lights and called them Stars. "Let them be lights in the heavens to separate Day from Night! Let them be signs to mark out the seasons, the days, and the years! Let them shine in Heaven to give light upon the Earth!" said God.

And so it was. God saw that it was good. It was the fourth day.

"Now," said God, "I will make the living beings that will live on Earth. Let the waters and land swarm with creatures that swim, or fly, or crawl." God created fishes and birds and all sorts of creeping animals.

"The plants have seeds," said God, "so I will give the living beings seeds, too. Now, they also can multiply and fill the land, seas, and sky with life." Presently the world teemed with countless beings, big and little, and of all kinds. It was the fifth day.

Dawn came. God saw that there were too few creatures living on the land. So God brought forth many more kinds of animals — cows and horses, lions and tigers, snakes and lizards — to walk and run upon the land. Then God blessed them and saw that it was good.

Still the world seemed a bit incomplete. What was missing? The Spirit of God looked deep into the mirrorlike waters. What God saw reflected back was an image. It was an image of God's own being.

"I know," God said. "We'll make creatures with spirits much like our own. They will care for all the plants and animals of the world."

God commanded, "Let the Earth bring forth man and woman."

With that, God formed two human beings from the dust and breathed life into them. The first people had been created.

God blessed them and said, "Be fruitful, and multiply. I have made the world for you, and you are to look after it." It was the sixth day.

God had finished the work of making the world. It had everything. Light and Darkness. Heaven above Earth. Sun and Moon and Stars. And on the Earth, there were Land and Seas. There were living Plants and Animals — all with seeds. And there was Woman and there was Man.

Everything in the Universe was as the Creator had willed it. Nothing unnecessary. Nothing missing. All perfectly in balance and in harmony.

God saw everything and behold, it was very good. With an uplifted spirit, God blessed the seventh day and declared it holy. It was Shabbat, the Sabbath. "It is a day of rest," proclaimed God.

Now the Spirit of the Sabbath came before God.

"God, you created all things in pairs," the Sabbath spoke. "Only me, you created single."

And God answered: "One day each week the Children of Israel will welcome you as a bride. Each week you will come as an honored guest for a one-day visit. In your honor, they will put on their finest clothes and serve their best food. When you are ready to depart, they will give you a heartfelt farewell — for each week you shall give them a foretaste of the peace and glory of the world to come."

And so it was. From then until today, the Jewish people are wedded to the Bride, Sabbath.

The basic story was adapted from the Bible, Book of Genesis, Chapters 1 and 2.

WHAT WE CELEBRATE

SHABBAT, HEBREW FOR THE "SABBATH," celebrates God's creation of the world and God's day of rest from that act. It is the most important holiday in the life of a Jew. The holiday reminds the Jewish people to rest on Shabbat, just as God rested on the seventh day.

Shabbat begins at sundown each Friday evening and ends when the first three stars appear Saturday evening. The day is one of peace and rest for all, even for the animals who pull the plows in the fields. It is also a time to freshen and restore the spirit. Jews observe the holiday every week of the year, some say, because their life on Earth is a continuous process of creation.

No one knows when Shabbat was first celebrated. Many think it grew from people's observations of the four phases of the moon every month — new, first half, full, last half. But on one point everyone agrees: Shabbat is the oldest and most sacred holiday of the year.

Shabbat is the only holiday set down in the Ten Commandments. The Fourth Commandment says, "You shall remember the Sabbath day and keep it holy." The wise rabbis of old said, "As Israel has kept the Sabbath so did the Sabbath keep Israel alive." Even very poor Jews will struggle all week in order to honor Shabbat with candles, wine, and proper food. Shabbat gives people time to relax and enjoy a taste of the world to come.

HOW WE CELEBRATE

THE HOLIDAY BEGINS AT SUNDOWN Friday evening with the blessing of Shabbat candles. The candles represent the freedom and light that

Shabbat brings to the human spirit. The sages tell us that the daily soul leaves, and a more loving and happy Shabbat soul enters each person for the day of peace.

Observant Jews greet the Sabbath Bride with prayer and song in the synagogue. Later, they begin a festive Shabbat meal in the home. The table is set with a clean white tablecloth and the best silver and china.

An adult recites the blessing called the *kiddush* over a full cup of wine, a symbol of joy. The kiddush recalls the completion of creation on the seventh day and the spiritual blessing of Shabbat. Then someone cuts or breaks the *challah*, a twisted egg bread that is eaten on Shabbat. Each person eats a piece and says a blessing with words praising God, "who brings bread out of the earth."

The traditional Shabbat meal usually includes fish, along with some special dishes. *Kugel*, a round noodle pudding, symbolizes the wish for a round, good week. Another favorite is *cholent*, a mixture of potatoes, peas, beans, and meat. Both dishes are cooked on Friday, before Shabbat, and left on the stove to stay warm for the rest of the holiday. In not cooking on Shabbat, Jews are imitating God who rested from all work on that day. The family sings *zemiroth*, table songs, between courses and after the meal.

On Saturday, many Jews attend services at the synagogue in the morning. Families lunch at home and study at the synagogue, or relax with relatives and friends during the afternoon. Time spent praying, eating, and talking together adds festivity and joy to Shabbat.

At the end of the day, people gather for the ceremony of *havdalah*, which is Hebrew for "separation." It marks the departure of the Sabbath Bride. A decorated box filled with aromatic spices is passed around and sniffed, to symbolize the wish for a fragrant week. Blessings over a glass filled to the brim with wine express the hope for a prosperous week to come. Finally a special candle is lit, made of many wicks twisted together. Everyone cups hands near the light to see the separation between light and dark. According to tradition, the separation is like the break between Shabbat and the workaday week.

An adult chants a prayer and puts out the flame by dipping it in the wine or pouring the wine on the wick over a havdalah dish. The mood is a little somber. The Sabbath Bride and the Sabbath souls are leaving. But the sad feeling does not last very long. Shabbat will be back in just six days. Everyone wishes one another *shavua tov,* Hebrew for a "good week," or *gute voch* in Yiddish!

CRAFTS AND FOOD

SHABBAT CANDLESTICKS • *All ages.*

Your family may have beautiful Shabbat candlesticks that were passed down from grandparents, received as gifts, or bought. If not, here is how to make very simple but attractive candleholders. Remember to light at least two candles. Some families like to kindle two lights for the parents and one light for each of the children.

YOU'LL NEED:

2 OR MORE EMPTY SPICE BOTTLES

SALT OR DRY SAND

SHABBAT CANDLES

METAL TRAY OR ALUMINUM FOIL

1. Discard covers and sifters of bottles.
2. Remove labels and wash bottles with soap and water until they're clean and sparkling. Let them dry.
3. Fill bottles nearly to the top with salt or dry sand.
4. Push the bottom of the Shabbat candles down into the salt or sand so that they remain erect.
5. Arrange candlesticks on a metal tray or on a surface with aluminum foil.

SPICE BOX • *All ages—with adult help.*

Havdalah spice boxes can be made of wood, clay, silver, or gold. The designs are often very intricate and delicate. But spice boxes can also be made of very simple materials, such as a beautiful orange studded with cloves. Here's a way to make your own spice box out of an egg carton.

YOU'LL NEED:

1 EGG CARTON

CINNAMON, CLOVES, AND ALLSPICE

GLUE OR TAPE

SMALL NAIL OR PENCIL

PAINT, CRAYONS, FELT PENS, GLITTER, STICKERS, RIBBONS, OR CREPE PAPER

1. Cut out 2 cups from the bottom of the egg carton.
2. Fill 1 cup with cinnamon, cloves, and allspice. Glue (or tape) the other cup on top.
3. Ask an adult to help poke holes in the top cup with a small nail or pencil.
4. Decorate your spice box with the craft materials.

KUGEL • *All ages — with adult help.*

YOU'LL NEED:

LARGE BOWL

MEASURING CUP AND SPOONS

WOODEN MIXING SPOON

GREASED ROUND CASSEROLE DISH, ABOUT 9 INCHES IN DIAMETER

16 OUNCES BROAD EGG NOODLES

1 STICK BUTTER OR MARGARINE

$\frac{1}{4}$ CUP SUGAR

2 LARGE EGGS, LIGHTLY BEATEN

$\frac{1}{2}$ TEASPOON CINNAMON

2 APPLES CUT INTO SMALL CHUNKS

$\frac{3}{4}$ CUP ORANGE JUICE

JUICE OF $\frac{1}{2}$ LEMON

$\frac{1}{2}$ TO 1 CUP RAISINS

1. Preheat oven to 325 degrees Fahrenheit.
2. Cook noodles according to directions on the package. Drain and place in a large bowl.
3. Add butter or margarine. Stir until it melts.
4. Add sugar, eggs, and cinnamon.
5. Add apples, juices, and raisins. Mix gently.
6. Pour into greased casserole dish. Bake for 1½ to 2 hours, depending on crustiness desired. Eat warm or cold.

Serves 6.

Rosh Hashanah

THE BINDING OF ISAAC

"THE FIRST DAY OF THE SEVENTH MONTH

SHALL BE A SOLEMN REST TO YOU,

A MEMORIAL PROCLAIMED WITH THE

BLOWING OF THE TRUMPETS."

Leviticus 23:24

LONG, LONG AGO, ON THE EASTERN COAST of the Mediterranean Sea there was a land called Canaan. Here lived Abraham, the head of a large clan of Hebrews.

The Hebrews were like members of a big family. And Abraham was their father. All believed that Abraham was the first person to worship only one god. "There is one God," Abraham said. "One God who created the Heaven and the Earth."

Abraham was a rich man with large flocks of sheep and herds of cattle. Yet he was very kind and generous. People said his tent had four doors so that a traveler coming from any direction could easily enter his home.

One hot, sunny day, Abraham sat quietly resting near his tent. He was then ninety-nine years old. His wife, Sarah, who was ninety years old, sat inside.

Suddenly Abraham looked up and saw three strangers approaching. The kindly old man sprang to his feet. Bowing low, he welcomed them.

"Come and rest a while in the shade of this tree. I see that you are tired. Let me fetch water and something for you to eat."

The men sat down. Abraham went into the tent to prepare food and drink. Although rich, he was not proud. He served the three visitors himself.

After eating, one of the men asked Abraham, "Where is Sarah, your wife?"

Abraham was stunned. How did this newcomer know his wife's name was Sarah?

"She is there, in the tent," he answered quietly.

All at once, a strange feeling came over Abraham. His hands trembled and his knees felt weak. The stranger's voice was familiar. Abraham remembered having heard it before. Could it be the voice of God?

Long before, in a dreamy mist, God had appeared in front of Abraham. A blinding light had ripped open the sky. The air rang with God's solemn voice. "I will bless your wife, Sarah, and I will give you a son by her," God told Abraham. "And you will name your son Isaac." Then the mist had lifted and the light dimmed. Abraham returned to his work and nothing more had happened. Yet Abraham never doubted God's word.

The visitor continued. "The three of us will be passing this way again in about a year. By that time your wife, Sarah, shall have a son."

Abraham was struck speechless. There could be no question. He was hearing the voice of God.

At this moment, Sarah stepped out of the tent. She had heard the stranger, and she burst out laughing. Bear a child at her age? How ridiculous! Surely everyone knew that she was too old to have children.

The stranger went up to Sarah. "Why did you laugh?" he asked kindly. "Is there anything too hard for God to do?"

Sarah grew frightened. She thought that she might have shown too little faith in God. She murmured, "I didn't laugh."

"Oh, yes, you did," he said, smiling gently.

The men bid Abraham and Sarah good-bye, and Abraham went along to show them the way. In a while, he returned home alone.

Almost a year later, it happened. Just as the visitor had said, Sarah bore a baby boy.

Sarah could not believe her miraculous good fortune. Her son was her greatest blessing. "The child is so bright and cheerful," she said to Abraham. "What shall we call him?"

Abraham remembered God's words. "Let us call him Isaac. It is a name that means laughter."

Sarah said, "It is a good name. This bundle of joy has made me laugh. Everyone who hears about Isaac will laugh with me!"

Many seasons passed. Isaac grew into a fine young man. Sarah and Abraham thanked God every day for their wonderful son and their newfound happiness.

One day, when Isaac was about eleven years old, God came to Abraham again. Out of a heavy mist, the grave voice intoned, "Abraham."

The aged leader dropped to his knees. "*Hineini*, Here I am," he replied.

God said, "Take your son, Isaac, whom you love, and go to the land of Moriah. Make him an offering upon a mountain you will find there."

Abraham's heart was heavy indeed. He bowed his head low and sighed deeply. Give up his beloved son? What was God asking? God had promised that many people would come from Abraham's family. How could this happen if Isaac died while still a boy?

The old man grew very pale. But he did not complain or argue. In his heart, he trusted God and believed in God's goodness.

Sarah saw her husband stooped over. She hurried to his side. "Husband," she cried. "What is the matter? Your face is so sorrowful and drained of color."

Abraham stood up and took the hand of his beautiful wife whom he loved so deeply.

"I have to go on a journey," he said softly. "There I will make a special offering to God who gave us our son, Isaac." Abraham paused. "I will take the boy with me," he said. "Also, two of our servants."

Sarah fell back, startled. "Why must you take the boy?" She scarcely breathed. Abraham did not know how to answer. So he simply said, "Because I must."

Early the next morning, Abraham rose and woke Isaac. Then he saddled his ass. With the help of the servants, they packed food for the journey and wood for the offering. Finally they set off.

Isaac was very pleased to be going far away. He chattered the whole time. "It is my first long journey," he kept saying. "And I am so excited."

Old Abraham rode ahead, saying nothing. But Isaac did not seem to notice his father's silence.

The group traveled for three whole days. Finally they arrived at the base of a high mountain. Abraham dismounted.

"Stay here with the ass," he told the servants. "Isaac and I will go up the mountain to worship."

Turning to Isaac, Abraham said, "My son, you carry the wood for the offering. I will take the torch with the fire. I will also take the knife."

Isaac looked around. "Father," he said. "We have the wood and the fire. But where is the lamb to offer up to God?"

Abraham's warm, brown eyes met those of Isaac. "My son," he answered, "God will provide the lamb."

Father and son climbed steadily. At last, they came to a little clearing. Abraham stopped. In the middle of the clearing was a great stone with a flat top.

"Pile the wood on there," he told Isaac.

Isaac hesitated, but Abraham said, "Obey me without question, just as I obey God without question."

Isaac did as he was told. In a little while he was finished. His father embraced him.

Abraham prepared to offer his son to God. Lovingly, he guided his son to the large, flat stone. He bound Isaac's hands and feet with rope. And he laid the boy upon the wood. Isaac looked at his father with fear. But he kept silent, as his father had asked.

Abraham shuddered and began to pray. Then he raised high the knife in his right hand.

Suddenly a voice called out, "Abraham! Abraham! Lay not your hand against the boy." Abraham froze.

The voice continued, "I know now that you are a God-fearing man. You have not withheld from me your son, your only son."

Abraham dropped the knife. Tears streamed down his face as he leaned over and kissed his son. Swiftly the old man took Isaac down and undid the ropes that bound him.

Abraham glanced around. He saw a wondrous sight. "Look, my son," he said, pointing to a dense grove of shrubbery. "God has provided the offering. There in the thicket is a ram caught by his horns."

Together Abraham and Isaac slew the ram and offered it up to God.

Then God called out again to Abraham. "You shall be blessed because you have obeyed me. Your children and your children's children will multiply. And some day they will become as numerous as the stars in the sky and the sands of the sea."

Abraham bent very low to the God of Israel, the God of life. When he straightened his back, he reached for Isaac's hand. Then, side by side, the old man and his son walked down the mountain and returned home.

In time, Abraham died and was buried beside Sarah in the Cave of Machpelah, in Hebron. His son, Isaac, took his place as a leader of the Hebrews. After Isaac came Jacob, the grandson of Abraham. Jacob's name was changed to Israel, and his followers called themselves the Children of Israel, or Israelites. The land that God promised them became known as the Land of Israel.

The basic story was adapted from the Bible, Book of Genesis, Chapters 18, 21, and 22. These Torah portions are read on the two days of Rosh Hashanah.

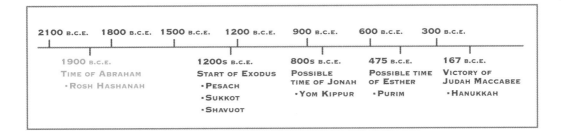

2100 B.C.E.	1800 B.C.E.	1500 B.C.E.	1200 B.C.E.	900 B.C.E.	600 B.C.E.	300 B.C.E.

1900 B.C.E.
TIME OF ABRAHAM
• ROSH HASHANAH

1200s B.C.E.
START OF EXODUS
• PESACH
• SUKKOT
• SHAVUOT

800s B.C.E.
POSSIBLE
TIME OF JONAH
• YOM KIPPUR

475 B.C.E.
POSSIBLE TIME
OF ESTHER
• PURIM

167 B.C.E.
VICTORY OF
JUDAH MACCABEE
• HANUKKAH

WHAT WE CELEBRATE

ROSH HASHANAH, HEBREW FOR "HEAD OF THE YEAR," celebrates the start of the Jewish year. On this day, it is said, Abraham offered to sacrifice his adored son. To sacrifice is to give up something for a very good reason. Abraham's sacrifice proved his faith in God. God allowed Abraham to kill a ram instead of Isaac. Thus, God's faith was also renewed in humankind.

Tradition tells us that Rosh Hashanah is the birthday of the world. On this day, God recalls the deeds — good and bad — of the people. And the people think back on how they behaved over the past year and how they could do better in the next one. Jews, therefore, do not greet the holiday with noisemakers and funny hats. Rather they approach it with a serious desire to make a fresh start in the new year.

Jews blow the *shofar*, Hebrew for "ram's horn," on Rosh Hashanah, unless the holiday falls on Shabbat. The horn is used because the ram was sacrificed instead of Isaac. The sound of the shofar reminds Jews that sacrifice is sometimes necessary. And it asks God, for Abraham's sake, to forgive their sins. The shofar is also used to awaken people's spirits and to call on them to repent. There are three basic shofar sounds: *tekiah*, a long plain note; *shevarim*, three broken notes; and *teruah*, a series of nine short blasts.

Were you mean to your brother or sister during the past year? Did you snub a friend? Did you neglect a relative? Rosh Hashanah begins the period called *teshuvah*, Hebrew for "returning [to God]," or Ten Days of Repentance. Now is the time to tell people you have hurt that you are sorry and to ask for forgiveness.

Ten days after the first day of Rosh Hashanah is the solemn festival of Yom Kippur. Together, the two celebrations are commonly called the High Holidays.

HOW WE CELEBRATE

LEGEND TELLS US THAT GOD opens the Book of Life on Rosh Hashanah. God judges each person and writes down his or her fate for the next year. For those who truly repent their sins, God shows mercy. The record is open until sundown on Yom Kippur. That's why Jews send cards to each other before Rosh Hashanah that read, "*L'shanah tovah tikatevu*, May you be inscribed in the Book of Life for a good year."

Jews observe Rosh Hashanah for one or two days, starting on the first days of the Jewish month of Tishri, which falls in September or October. Many people attend synagogue, dressed in their best for the holiday. Customarily, some wear white to symbolize purity and divine forgiveness. The prayers during this holiday are meant to ensure that one's name is included in the book of those who will survive the year.

People eat special sweet foods on Rosh Hashanah. The festive meal usually begins with apple dipped in honey, a symbol of good luck and a sweet new year. The round, crownlike bread, or *challah*, stands for the endless cycles of the year or for the eternal rule of God. Other traditional Ashkenazic foods for Rosh Hashanah are honey pastries known as *teiglach*, honey cake, and *tzimmes*, a dish made from carrots and sweet potatoes. It is the custom among Sephardim to eat a pear, plum, or other new fruit not yet eaten that season.

After the afternoon meal on the first day of Rosh Hashanah, Jews gather at a nearby river or other body of running water. In a ceremony called *tashlikh*, Hebrew for "you shall cast away," the people symbolically empty their pockets of bread crumbs. The crumbs they toss into the water represent the casting off of sins.

CRAFTS AND FOOD

ROSH HASHANAH CARDS

Making and sending cards to friends and relatives is a very special way to observe the High Holidays. The traditional message is, *"L'shanah tovah tikatevu,* May you be inscribed in the Book of Life for a good year."

CARD 1 • *All ages.*

YOU'LL NEED:

> 1 PIECE WHITE PAPER, 8½ INCHES BY 11 INCHES
>
> 1 SHEET TISSUE PAPER
>
> SCISSORS
>
> PASTE
>
> FELT PEN

1. Fold paper in half top to bottom, then in half left to right.
2. Cut out 2 triangles from tissue paper. Make each side about 3 inches long.
3. Paste 1 triangle on front of the twice-folded piece of paper. Paste other triangle upside down on top of the first to form a 6-pointed Star of David.
4. Write your message inside the folded card.

CARD 2 • *Ages 8 and up.*

YOU'LL NEED:

1 PIECE WHITE PAPER, 8½ INCHES BY 11 INCHES

SCISSORS

RULER

FELT PENS

1. Fold paper in half.
2. Cut out a square, 3 inches by 3 inches, from both top right-hand corners. Discard 2 square scraps.
3. Fold top part of card over and down to the right at an angle so that the 2 cut edges align. Make a sharp crease along the fold.
4. Lift up flap and open card flat. Fold card in the opposite direction along center crease. Open card flat again. Pinch center sections with your fingers as you close the card.
5. Write your new year message inside the part that pops up, and decorate your card.

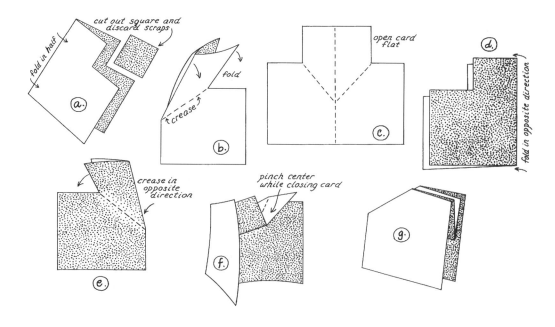

CARD 3 • *Ages 8 and up.*

YOU'LL NEED:

INDEX CARD

SCISSORS

1 PIECE WHITE PAPER, 8$\frac{1}{2}$ INCHES BY 11 INCHES

TEMPERA PAINT

SMALL PAINTBRUSH

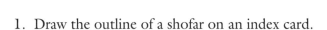

1. Draw the outline of a shofar on an index card.
2. Carefully cut out the shofar and set it aside. It is your stencil.
3. Fold paper in half from top to bottom and then in half from left to right.
4. Place stencil on top of the twice-folded piece of paper.
5. Hold stencil in place while you paint around it with tempera paint.
6. Remove stencil.
7. Let paint dry and write your message inside and outside the card.

HONEY PLATE • *All ages — with adult help.*

On Rosh Hashanah, people dip pieces of apple into honey as a symbol of the sweet year to come. A honey plate makes a great holder for a bowl of honey.

YOU'LL NEED:

INEXPENSIVE SAUCER OR SMALL PLATE

FELT PEN

QUICK-DRYING PAINT

1. Draw designs on the plate with the felt pen. Torah scrolls, lions, a crown, flowers, a shofar, and the Star of David are all traditional symbols.

2. Paint the designs. Then let saucer dry fully.
3. Fill a clear bowl (not the painted plate) with honey.
4. Set honey bowl on decorated plate and use for dipping.

CHALLAH • *Ages 8 and up — with adult help.*

It is traditional to eat special, round loaves of challah at the Rosh Hashanah meal. Challah is also eaten on Shabbat and at all festivals, except Pesach.

YOU'LL NEED:

LARGE BOWL

WOODEN MIXING SPOON

MEASURING CUP AND SPOONS

LARGE CUTTING BOARD

CLEAN, DAMP TOWEL

LIGHTLY FLOURED BOARD

GREASED COOKIE SHEET

2 TABLESPOONS DRY YEAST

$\frac{1}{3}$ CUP WARM WATER

$\frac{2}{3}$ CUP HOT WATER

1 TEASPOON SALT

1 TABLESPOON SUGAR

$\frac{1}{4}$ CUP OIL

3 EGGS

$3\frac{1}{2}$ CUPS FLOUR

1. Dissolve yeast in warm water in large bowl.
2. Add salt and sugar and stir.
3. Beat 2 eggs and oil together. Slowly add to yeast mixture.
4. Add 3 cups flour and $\frac{2}{3}$ cup hot water slowly. Stir until dough forms a ball.
5. Sprinkle large cutting board with half of remaining flour and place dough on top.
6. Knead for about 10 minutes until dough does not stick to board or hand.
7. Place dough back in bowl and cover with a clean, damp towel.
8. Let dough rise for about 2 hours or until it doubles in size.
9. Put dough back on lightly floured board and knead for about 1 minute.
10. Roll dough into a long snake about 18 inches long. Form dough into a flat spiral on a greased cookie sheet. Press end against spiral and seal it with a little water.
11. Place dough spiral on baking sheet and let rise for another 45 minutes.
12. Preheat oven to 375 degrees Fahrenheit.
13. Brush top of dough spiral with 1 beaten egg.
14. Bake for 40 minutes.
15. Remove challah to rack to cool.

Makes 1 round bread.

Yom Kippur

JONAH AND THE GREAT FISH

"THE TENTH DAY OF THIS SEVENTH MONTH SHALL BE YOUR DAY OF ATONEMENT,

A DAY . . . WHEN YOU SHALL SEARCH YOUR SOULS.

YOU SHALL DO NO MANNER OF WORK ON THAT DAY,

FOR IT IS A DAY WHEN YOU MAKE ATONEMENT BEFORE GOD."

Leviticus 23:27

THERE ONCE LIVED A MAN NAMED JONAH. He was a farmer in the northern kingdom of Israel. But Jonah was no ordinary farmer. He was a prophet, someone who can speak the word of God.

One day, Jonah lay resting after a hard day's work. Suddenly he heard a loud, booming voice. He knew the sound. It was God's voice.

"Arise, Jonah," God thundered. "Go at once to the great Assyrian city of Nineveh. The people there have become evil and wicked. Tell them they have forty days to mend their ways. If not, I will destroy them and their city."

Jonah was a wise man. But he was also very stubborn. Above all else, he loved to argue. So he cast his eyes heavenward.

"Why did you pick me, God?" Jonah protested. "Why not someone else? The people of Nineveh will not listen to me."

Jonah waited. But God did not reply. So Jonah went on. "Besides, Nineveh is very far away. Those people are my enemies. They worship idols and false gods. I have no desire to save them. Let them die without warning!"

Jonah's words simply echoed in the valley. "And there is something else," he continued. "How do I know you will really punish the people of Nineveh? You may end up being kind and forgiving. Perhaps you'll even pardon them for the bad things they have done."

Jonah heard not another word from God. God's order stood. So Jonah decided to run away. He would flee rather than bring God's message to the people of Nineveh.

Jonah quickly threw a few possessions into a bag. He climbed onto the back of his donkey and rode off.

Along the way, Jonah passed through the port city of Jaffa. Suddenly he got an idea. He went to the docks. There he found a ship about to set sail. "Where are you going?" he asked the captain.

"To Tarshish," the man replied.

Jonah could not believe his luck. He could book passage and sail to the far-off city. God would never find him on the vast ocean waters that separated Jaffa from Tarshish.

"Wait for me," Jonah told the captain. "I'll be right back." He ran to the marketplace and sold his donkey. With the money, he paid the captain for his journey and went aboard.

The ship set sail. It glided smoothly through the calm seas. That night, the weary Jonah went below deck and fell into a deep sleep.

Suddenly a terrible storm broke loose. The darkness was shattered by flashes of lightning. The silence of the sea gave way to the roar of thunder. Gusts of wind tore the sails to tatters. Huge waves battered the decks and cracked the masts.

The terrified captain gathered his crew together. Each man came from a different nation and believed in a different god.

"This storm must have been sent by the gods!" the captain shouted. "They must be angry at one of us. Let us each pray to our own gods to end the storm."

So the men did. But the storm raged on.

Then the sailors thought to lighten the load so the ship would not sink. They flung cargo overboard. But still the timbers of the hull shook violently. The boat seemed close to breaking apart.

All at once, the captain remembered Jonah. He rushed below and awoke his dozing passenger. "How can you sleep so soundly?" the captain called. "Get up on deck!"

As Jonah came up on deck, the sailors eyed him suspiciously. "Someone has brought the storm upon us," they cried. "Come. Let us draw lots to see who is guilty."

Each one drew a number. The captain gathered together the papers. His stern glance passed over every member of his crew. Then his blazing eyes rested on Jonah.

"Your number is the lowest!" the captain snapped.

The sailors pointed to him. "It is you, Jonah! You have brought this misfortune upon us. Who are you? What have you done?"

Jonah felt heartsick. Even here on the open sea, God had found him. It was time to cast aside all thoughts of escape. He confessed everything.

"I am a Hebrew," Jonah replied. "Like my people, I worship only one God. But I did something terribly wrong. I disobeyed God's command."

The sailors were quiet. Then someone asked, "But what must we do to calm the sea?"

"Cast me overboard," Jonah groaned. "This terrible storm came because of what I did."

The sailors did not move. None of them wanted to harm Jonah. So the captain ordered the sailors to row harder. They tried, but the sea was too rough. And the storm grew worse and worse.

After some time, the terrified sailors stopped rowing. They prayed again to their gods. "Please do not let us die because of this man," they pleaded.

The captain strode across the lurching ship. "Jonah!" he shouted. "We have no choice. If we do not toss you overboard, all of us will perish."

Without complaining, Jonah stretched out his arms. The sailors took hold of him and flung him into the savage sea.

Instantly the storm ended. The sky cleared. A gentle breeze blew up. And the ship sailed on.

Jonah drifted alone in the deep ocean waters. "Oh, God, what now?" he implored.

Strong currents swirled around him. And swift waters carried him along. They pulled him toward the cavelike mouth of a huge fish. Before Jonah knew it, he was deep inside the fish's belly!

Jonah spoke humbly. "Dear God, please save me. I know that I have brought these troubles on myself. But I am truly grateful for all the good things you have given me. I promise now to do as I am told."

Jonah could not be sure God heard his words. But after three days and three nights the fish opened its mouth. With a giant heave, it tossed Jonah out. He fell upon dry land.

Now God spoke a second time. "Go at once to Nineveh," God ordered.

This time Jonah did not argue. He set out directly for the distant city of Nineveh. Jonah would bring the people God's warning — even though he still did not want God to forgive them.

Nineveh was an enormous city. Jonah walked everywhere crying aloud the message of God. "People of Nineveh!" he shouted. "You have grown wicked and evil. You have forty days to repent. If not, you and your city shall be destroyed!"

Jonah's voice reached every corner of the great city. The people listened to what Jonah said. They grew very frightened.

Finally the king of Nineveh heard Jonah's warning. "It is true," the king said. "I have ruled badly. The people have become evil and corrupt. It is time to change. Maybe God will forgive us."

The king came down from his golden throne. He took off his purple robes and put on rough sackcloth. On his head, he scattered ashes in place of his crown.

The king then issued orders for all the people of Nineveh. "Go without food or drink for forty days. Dress in sackcloth and rub yourself with ashes. Stop your cruel and dishonest ways. Pray for forgiveness."

Everyone obeyed. Not only did they fast and pray, but they also did good deeds. They confessed their secret crimes and sins aloud, even if it meant certain punishment.

At the end of forty days, the people of Nineveh were worn out. But their joy was great. Seeing that they had had a real change of heart, God pardoned them and spared their city.

All the people celebrated — except Jonah. He rushed out of the city and sat down on a stone in the hot sun. Bitterly, he quarreled with God.

"I knew that you were too loving and merciful to destroy Nineveh," he said. "That's why I disobeyed you. Please, God, take my life. I want to die."

God answered Jonah with a question. "Do you think it is right for you to be so angry about Nineveh?"

Jonah did not answer. He just sulked. Day after day, he sat in the hot sun hoping that God would destroy Nineveh.

Then one morning, Jonah awoke and saw something wonderful. God had made a large tree grow up next to him. The tree offered him shade and protection.

All day long, Jonah sat in the tree's shade. The giant leaves protected him from the heat of the sun. He welcomed the coolness the tree brought.

That night, Jonah slept very well. But when he awoke the next morning, he saw that something horrible had occurred. A giant worm had killed the tree! It was all dried and withered.

Right away, Jonah called on God. "God," he asked crossly, "why did you send a worm to attack the tree? Poor tree! How I pity it."

God waited a moment and then spoke. "Do you think it is right for you to be angry about the death of the tree?"

"I certainly do," Jonah replied.

Then God said, "You feel sorry for the tree, though it lived for only one day. You didn't plant it or care for it. But I made the people of Nineveh and watched over them for thousands of years. Yes, they were slow to learn right from wrong. Yet, I pity them."

Jonah wept with shame. Now he understood something important. God loved all people and believed in the power of human beings to change. God was concerned with how we learn from our mistakes and try always to improve ourselves.

The remorseful Jonah kneeled down. In a strong voice, he prayed. "Dear God, I sincerely regret what I have said and done. Please forgive me."

God blessed Jonah and accepted his prayer. Jonah had learned the importance of true repentance and the mercy of God, the reason for Yom Kippur.

The basic story was adapted from the Bible, Book of Jonah, Chapters 1 through 4. The Book of Jonah is read on the afternoon of Yom Kippur.

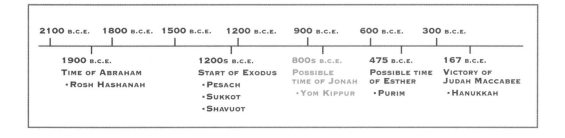

WHAT WE CELEBRATE

YOM KIPPUR, HEBREW FOR "DAY OF ATONEMENT," is the holiest and most solemn holiday of the Jewish year. It marks the end of a ten-day period of repentance, sometimes called the Days of Awe. The festival starts on the evening of the ninth day of Tishri, which falls in September or October. The holiday ends the following evening, just after the first three stars can be seen in the sky.

Yom Kippur is a time for thinking about *teshuvah*, returning to the right path. On this day, legend tells us, the gates of Heaven are open wide and all thoughts and prayers fly right to God. According to custom, on Yom Kippur Jews reach out to those they may have hurt or those who may have hurt them and ask forgiveness. Did you tell a lie or do something else that you know was wrong? This is the time to tell the person you are sorry and to think how you can change in the year ahead.

It is always good to give money or *tzedakah*, Hebrew for "charity," to the poor. But it is especially important to do so before Yom Kippur. Tzedakah and teshuvah are the two main points of the holiday.

Jews read from the Book of Jonah during Yom Kippur because it emphasizes repentance. Just as Jonah asked God to forgive him for running away, Jews ask God to forgive them for their misdeeds and wrongdoings. And just as God showed Jonah pity when he repented, Jews hope God will be kind and compassionate when they show that they are truly sorry and try to improve themselves.

But the story of Jonah brings other messages as well. It teaches that God is everywhere and people cannot flee God or God's commandments. And it tells us, too, that it is important for people to live in peace with themselves, with their fellow human beings, and with the rest of God's creatures.

HOW WE CELEBRATE

FOR MANY PEOPLE, Yom Kippur starts the day before the holiday with a large meal in the late afternoon. A favorite first dish is *kreplach*, dough filled with meat, similar to wonton or tortellini, and served floating in chicken soup. The kreplach can also be fried and served as a side dish. The meat is said to symbolize God's stern justice, and the soft dough that covers the meat denotes God's compassion. You can also replace the meat with potato or kasha. The main dish is usually poultry.

Jews generally light *yahrzeit*, Yiddish for "anniversary," candles at sunset on Yom Kippur eve. Each candle is in memory of a loved one who died. Then it's off to synagogue. The greeting used during this day is "*Gemar hatimah tovah!* May you be sealed for good in the Book of Life!"

For many, the high point of the Yom Kippur eve service comes just before sunset. It is the singing of the *Kol Nidre*, "all vows." This prayer asks pardon for all unfulfilled promises made to God.

The day of Yom Kippur is a time for fasting — except for children under the age of thirteen and those who are sick or weak. Not eating and being hungry makes people think of those who don't have enough food. It reminds them to help others. The rabbis say that after people eat, they have but one heart, for themselves alone. But when people fast, they have two hearts, one for themselves, and one for all hungry people.

Those who attend religious services spend Yom Kippur praying, confessing their sins, asking forgiveness, and listening to traditional Torah readings. Part of the Yom Kippur service is a prayer for the dead called *Yizkor*, Hebrew for "remember." As the sun sets, people offer their last prayers. The service closes with the *Neilah*, Hebrew for "closing [of the gates]," and a last appeal for God's mercy. The blast of the *shofar*, or ram's horn, signals the final sealing of the heavenly gates.

Yom Kippur is over. It's time to eat. Jews break the fast of Yom Kippur with a light meal. They join friends and family to celebrate the start of a happy new year. Then it's outdoors to hammer in the first post for the *sukkah*, an outdoor booth, and a reminder of God's protection. The sukkah marks the start of the next holiday, Sukkot, and the continuity of the Jewish year. What a good way to end Yom Kippur!

CRAFTS AND FOOD

YAHRZEIT CANDLE • *Ages 8 and up — with adult help.*

It is the custom to light the yahrzeit candle for a near relative on the eve of Yom Kippur. You can make your own with candle wax and wick from a crafts store.

Note: Paraffin wax catches fire if it gets too hot. Drips of hot wax can burn your skin.

YOU'LL NEED:

> **SEVERAL CHUNKS PARAFFIN WAX**
>
> **8-INCH CANDLEWICK**
>
> **SMALL, EMPTY CAN**
>
> **SAUCEPAN**

1. Fill saucepan with about 2 inches of water and heat it over low heat on the stove.
2. Put a few chunks of paraffin into can, and place can into water.
3. Let paraffin melt slowly. Add more paraffin if you wish to make a very big candle.
4. Slowly lower wick down into the liquid wax. Then slowly lift the wick out. Hold it until wax begins to cool and get solid.
5. Repeat step 4, over and over, until candle gets fatter and will fit snugly inside an empty can.
6. Hang candle by wick end to cool.
7. Trim off extra wick.

YAHRZEIT CANDLEHOLDER • *Ages 8 and up — with adult help.*
Set the yahrzeit candle inside the yahrzeit candleholder and light it at
sunset on Yom Kippur eve.

YOU'LL NEED:
> **CANDLE**
>
> **EMPTY CAN**
>
> **WATER**
>
> **HAMMER**
>
> **LARGE NAIL**

1. Peel off label and clean can inside and out.
2. Fill can almost to the top with water and place it in the freezer until water is
   frozen. (The purpose is to make the can stiff.)
3. Ask an adult to help you make a pattern of holes all around can with a
   hammer and a large nail. The holes will allow the candlelight to show
   through. If you want, you can make holes in the shape of the Star of David.
4. Place can in the sink until ice melts and pour out water.
5. Set candle in can before lighting.

KREPLACH • *Ages 8 and up — with adult help.*
Kreplach are triangular-shaped dumplings that are often eaten before
the fast of Yom Kippur.

YOU'LL NEED:
> **MIXING BOWL**
>
> **ROLLING PIN**
>
> **FLOURED BOARD**
>
> **WOODEN MIXING SPOON**

CLEAN, DAMP TOWEL

POT WITH BOILING CHICKEN SOUP OR SALT WATER

MEASURING CUP AND SPOONS

$\frac{1}{4}$ CUP VEGETABLE OIL

2 TEASPOONS SALT

1 CUP WARM WATER

4 CUPS ALL-PURPOSE FLOUR

1 POUND GROUND MEAT SEASONED WITH SALT AND PEPPER

1. Mix oil, salt, and warm water in bowl.
2. Stir in flour.
3. Knead dough until smooth and soft and form into a ball. Divide ball into 2 parts, and cover 1 part with a damp cloth or towel.
4. Roll uncovered ball of dough out on floured board until it is $\frac{1}{8}$-inch-thick rectangle, about 10 inches by 12 inches. Cut into 30 2-inch squares.
5. Place a teaspoon of meat onto each square.
6. Dip your fingers in flour. Fold up the edges of the dough and press them together to form a triangle. Let stand for about 10 minutes.
7. Repeat steps 4, 5, and 6 with second ball of dough.
8. Drop kreplach into boiling soup or salt water and cook for 30 minutes.
9. Serve in soup, or remove from broth and brown for 10 minutes in a 375-degree-Fahrenheit oven.
10. 3 kreplach make 1 serving.

Makes about 60 kreplach.

BREAK-THE-FAST MEAL OF YOM KIPPUR • *All ages.*
Families and friends gather at the end of Yom Kippur to break the fast together. The foods they eat vary widely, but the feeling is always warm and personal.

Typically, the table is laden with a selection of different dairy dishes, such as herring, whitefish salad, devilled eggs, thinly sliced smoked salmon, sliced cheese, black olives, and cherry tomatoes. The breads can include challah, bagels, and pita.

FRUITS IN SYRUP • *Ages 8 and up — with adult help.*

The first fruits of the season cooked in syrup are a popular Sephardic dessert for the end of Yom Kippur. This dish can be made a few days in advance of the holiday.

YOU'LL NEED:

1 CUP SUGAR	SAUCEPAN
3 CUPS WATER	WOODEN MIXING SPOON
1 TEASPOON CINNAMON	MEASURING CUP
$^1/_4$ TEASPOON GROUND CLOVES	AND SPOONS
JUICE OF 1 LEMON	PEELER
8 FIRM APPLES, PEARS, OR PLUMS	SHARP KNIFE
2 TEASPOONS VANILLA	GLASS BOWL

1. Combine sugar, water, cinnamon, cloves, and lemon juice in a large saucepan. Bring to a boil, stirring constantly.
2. Boil mixture for 15 minutes. Lower heat to simmer.
3. Peel fruits. Cut into quarters and remove cores.
4. Add fruit to saucepan. Cook for 7 minutes.
5. Remove saucepan from heat. Stir in vanilla.
6. Transfer to glass bowl and store in refrigerator.

Serves 6.

Sukkot

THE LONG JOURNEY

"ON THE FIFTEENTH DAY OF THIS SEVENTH MONTH
IS THE FEAST OF TABERNACLES . . . ALL WHO ARE ISRAELITES
SHALL DWELL IN BOOTHS, THAT YOUR GENERATION MAY KNOW
THAT I MADE THE CHILDREN OF ISRAEL DWELL IN BOOTHS
WHEN I BROUGHT THEM OUT OF THE LAND OF EGYPT."

Leviticus 23:34

MOSES, THE LEADER OF THE ISRAELITES, had freed his people from slavery in Egypt. He had helped them to cross the Red Sea. Now he was taking them across the desert wilderness. Eventually they would reach Canaan — the land of their ancestors.

Late one afternoon, Moses halted the long, slow-moving caravan of men and women, children, donkeys, sheep, and cattle. "Here is a good place to camp for the night," he said.

With loud sighs, the people dropped their bundles on the desert sand. They unloaded the small tabernacles, called *sukkot*, that they carried. These wooden booths sheltered the Israelites at night. During the day, the sukkot protected the people from the blazing sun.

There was little laughter or happiness among the Children of Israel. The food that they had brought out of Egypt was all gone. The goatskins, in which they had been carrying their supply of water, were empty.

Two brothers pushed through the crowd looking for Moses. Finally they found him. One brother addressed Moses crossly.

"Our mother is weak. She is worn out from walking under the burning sun all day. Can you help us?"

Moses was distressed. What could he do? He loved his people. He wished to make them happy. Taking them out of Egypt had raised their hopes and spirits. But trekking through the hot wilderness was making them bitter and angry.

"Go to your mother," Moses said gently. "Remind her that God protects us. God delivered us from Egypt. God will bring us to Canaan. Tell her to trust God."

The brothers grumbled, but went away. Soon others approached the tall, elderly leader.

"Why did you take us out of Egypt?" a grizzled old man asked Moses. "Our lives as slaves were hard. But at least there we had food to eat and water to drink. In this wilderness, we have nothing but hunger and thirst."

Moses tried to comfort him. He said, "Remember, you are a free man now. Before you were a slave. Soon you will be in Canaan, the land of plenty that God has promised us. There you will find springs and trees, green fields and cool hills. Have faith. God will help us."

The old man returned to his family.

In the morning, the Israelites awoke in their booths. They picked up their packs and moved on.

After a while, they came to an oasis in the desert. Here at last they found water. It flowed from a hole in the ground. A few dashed forward to drink it. But they quickly spit it out.

"The water is bitter," a mother whined. "We cannot give it to our children."

Moses grieved. Heavy-hearted, he prayed to God to show him the way.

"Take a branch of that tree and fling it into the water," God said. "The branch will make the water pure."

Moses did as God commanded. He took a branch and threw it into the water. And the water became sweet and good. The people drank deeply and satisfied their thirst.

The Israelites marched on. They came to a spot where there were twelve springs of water and seventy palm trees. In this wonderful place, Moses and his followers camped beside the springs. How pleasant it was! In the evenings, the families gathered around and told stories of their ancestors, of Abraham and Sarah, of Isaac and Rebecca. They drank the water and refreshed themselves.

When they were rested, the Children of Israel and the animals pushed on. They walked from dawn to dark. At night, they camped inside their booths and tents.

But conditions got bad again. The Israelites complained to Moses. Quarrels arose. The protesting grew worse than before.

Once more Moses prayed to God. This time a dazzling light appeared all at once. It shone out of a cloud. The very heavens seemed to break open. The sky gleamed with rays as from a thousand suns.

God spoke to Moses. "*Hineini*, Here I am," the voice resounded. Moses stiffened. He knew these words. They were the same words Abraham used when called upon to sacrifice his son, Isaac.

"Tell the people that I have heard their complaints," God went on. "When the sun goes down they will have meat to eat. In the morning they will have bread. Then they will know that I am their God."

Moses told his people what God had said.

"How do we know this will really happen?" many grumbled.

They continued to complain until evening. Then, even the loudest among them grew quiet. As it got dark, a giant flock of birds, called quails, flew into the camp. The Israelites caught the birds and prepared the evening meals. Silently they ate and ate. That night everyone went to sleep with a full stomach.

By morning, however, they were hungry again. "Where is the bread you promised us?" several people asked Moses. "A wet dew is covering everything around the camp. It does not look at all like bread!"

Moses kept calm. He had perfect faith. "Just wait until the drops dry," he said.

Sure enough the dew dried. It left behind a thin, flaky, white coating that looked like frost. Some people tasted the bits. "Hmm," they murmured. "They taste sweet. Like crumbs covered with honey."

Happily the Children of Israel gathered the flakes. They asked one another, "What is it? What is it?" Before long they began to call it *manna*, the Hebrew word for "what is it?"

"This is the bread God has given you," Moses told his people. "But there is one rule from God you must follow. Each of you is to gather only as much as you need."

Every day the men and women arose early. They scooped up enough manna for their families. Only a few greedy ones took extra amounts. "We'll just put some away in case there is none tomorrow," they whispered.

Those who gathered too much manna were surprised at what they found the next morning. The extra manna had rotted! It was full of worms and smelled horrid.

Moses scolded them. "You doubted God. You gathered more than you should have," he said. "From now on, take only as much as you can eat."

The people obeyed, and both Moses and God forgave them.

On the sixth day, Moses told everyone, "Today, according to God's rule, you may take a double measure of manna. For tomorrow is Shabbat. It is a holy day of rest. You cannot gather manna tomorrow."

This time, too, a few people decided not to heed the words of Moses. "We see no reason not to gather manna on Shabbat," they muttered.

But the next day, there was no manna to be found. Only those who had gathered a double measure on the sixth day had enough to eat on Shabbat. Those who planned to gather manna on Shabbat went hungry.

More time passed. The earth was parched and once more the Israelites had no water to drink. "Our children and cattle are as dry as bone," they wailed.

Moses appealed again to God. "What can I do with those who still mistrust your gifts?" he asked.

"Take some of them with you," God told Moses. "Go to a rock where I will await you. Strike the rock with your staff. Water will overflow."

So it was. God led Moses to the rock. Moses brought his staff down hard. And the rock became a fountain! Water gushed out. There was plenty for everybody. The people gave thanks and continued on their way to the Promised Land.

It was then that more dreadful trouble struck. Moses and the Israelites came upon a fierce and warlike tribe of Amalekite nomads. These strangers surprised the followers of Moses with a sneak attack on their line of march. Many Israelites were killed.

Moses called over his lieutenant Joshua. "Gather together some men," Moses said. "We must fight the Amalekites."

To the troops, Moses said, "Fear not. We will conquer these enemies of Israel. I will stand on top of this hill overlooking the battlefield. In my hand I will hold the staff of God. It will protect you."

Joshua and his company of men got ready. They waited until the Amalekites surged forward. Then quickly they began hurling rocks and javelins at the approaching forces.

As long as Moses pointed his staff to Heaven, the Israelites were strong. They beat back the Amalekites. But when Moses let his hand drop, the Amalekites advanced.

All day long, the armies fought. "My arm grows weary," said Moses. "I can no longer hold it up to help my people."

Two soldiers were on the hill with Moses. They brought him a stone to sit on. Together they helped Moses hold aloft the staff of God. By the time the sun set, the battle was over. The Israelites had defeated the Amalekites.

Slowly, the weary Children of Israel packed up and continued on their way to Canaan. But now there was no complaining. Men, women, and children praised Moses. With uplifted hearts and minds, they began to speak of God's miracles.

Finally, after three months of wandering, the people reached a vast open plain. It was at the foot of a bare mountain known as Mount Sinai.

"This is the place," God told Moses, "where I will make the Children of Israel into a great nation."

Moses spoke with the people and they celebrated with song and dance. Young and old helped to unload the belongings. And each little group set up their wooden booths, their sukkot.

Everyone offered prayers of thanksgiving. They vowed always to remember how God had brought them to this place. Generation after generation would build sukkot in the autumn. For seven days they would live in huts decorated with green boughs and fruit. The huts would recall God's bounty and protection when their ancestors had dwelled in the wilderness.

The basic story was adapted from the Bible, Book of Exodus, Chapters 15 through 17, and Book of Leviticus, Chapter 23, which are read on Sukkot.

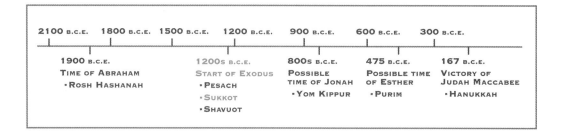

2100 B.C.E.	1800 B.C.E.	1500 B.C.E.	1200 B.C.E.	900 B.C.E.	600 B.C.E.	300 B.C.E.

1900 B.C.E.	1200s B.C.E.	800s B.C.E.	475 B.C.E.	167 B.C.E.
TIME OF ABRAHAM	START OF EXODUS	POSSIBLE TIME OF JONAH	POSSIBLE TIME OF ESTHER	VICTORY OF JUDAH MACCABEE
•ROSH HASHANAH	•PESACH	•YOM KIPPUR	•PURIM	•HANUKKAH
	•SUKKOT			
	•SHAVUOT			

WHAT WE CELEBRATE

THE FESTIVAL OF SUKKOT begins on the fifteenth day of the Hebrew month of Tishri, which falls in September or October, following Yom Kippur. Sukkot is the Hebrew word for "booths." The singular is *sukkah*. The holiday celebrates God's bounty in nature and God's protection, symbolized by the booths or tabernacles of the Israelites. The holiday, which lasts for seven days, is sometimes called the Festival of the Booths or the Feast of the Tabernacles. It is among the happiest of Jewish holidays.

People have long celebrated in the fall, when the crops are being harvested. Out of this tradition grew still another name for Sukkot — the Festival of In-Gathering. In-Gathering means harvesting the crops at the end of summer.

Thus, Sukkot commemorates both the Israelites' successful journey through the desert *and* the season when crops are gathered in. Farmers once built small, temporary houses in the fields to use during the harvest season. Today, the sukkot, or sukkahs, as they are sometimes called, not only remind Jews of the booths in which their ancestors had dwelled during the Exodus from Egypt, but they also call to mind the simple field huts of farmers. Sukkot is a joyous festival of thankfulness, similar to the American holiday of Thanksgiving.

How We Celebrate

Jewish families get ready for Sukkot by building a sukkah. They make the roof of leafy tree branches or wooden slats. It should protect the people within from the sun during the day. Yet it should let the people inside see the stars at night.

During Sukkot many Jewish families eat, study, and relax in the sukkah instead of in their houses. The very devout sleep there. People usually decorate the sukkah with flowers, fruit, paper chains, and pictures of Jerusalem. It is the custom to invite guests into the sukkah to share meals. This tradition was inspired by Abraham who always invited strangers and passersby to eat at his table.

Many people observe Sukkot with joyous parades around the synagogue each day of the holiday, carrying four species of plants. One species is *etrog*, Hebrew for "citron," a fruit similar to a lemon. Branches of three trees — palm, myrtle, and willow — tied together make up the other three species, called *lulav*. Each day of the holiday (except for Shabbat), people shake the four species to celebrate God's bounty at the time of the harvest. Some say the four species symbolize the different types of people in the Jewish community — from spiritually strong to spiritually weak. Just as all four species are held together, so the community must be united, with people helping one another.

People wave lulav and point etrog in the four directions of the compass, as well as up and down, while they chant prayers. This is to show gratitude that God is to be found everywhere — north, south, east, west, in Heaven, and on Earth.

CRAFTS AND FOOD

FESTIVE CENTERPIECE • *All ages.*
Each evening of the holiday, family and guests gather in the sukkah for meals. A large plate or basket full of colorful fruits and vegetables can make a great centerpiece. Try combining pumpkins and squash with apples, pears, plums, and oranges.

WALL HANGING • *All ages — with adult help.*
A colorful banner hanging from the roof or a wall of the sukkah adds to the holiday spirit.

YOU'LL NEED:

> **COAT HANGER**
>
> **OLD SHEET OR PILLOWCASE**
>
> **PAINT**
>
> **STAPLER**

1. Measure width of coat hanger.
2. Cut an old sheet or pillowcase the same width as the hanger and as long as you like. Iron if necessary.
3. Paint a colorful picture or design on the cloth. Some traditional designs show flowers, fruit, or bunches of grapes. You can also make one that says, "*Baruch ha-ba*, Blessed be the one who comes."
4. Wrap top of cloth around the bottom of hanger and staple banner into place.
5. Find a good place in the sukkah to hang the banner.

HARVEST CASSEROLE • *Ages 8 and up — with adult help.*

This casserole contains several vegetables popular at the end of summer.

YOU'LL NEED:

LARGE SAUCEPAN

MEASURING CUP AND SPOONS

2-QUART CASSEROLE DISH

WOODEN MIXING SPOON

3 TABLESPOONS VEGETABLE OIL

1 CUP SLICED ONION

$\frac{1}{2}$ CUP CHOPPED MUSHROOMS

$3\frac{1}{2}$ CUPS VEGETABLE BROTH

$1\frac{1}{2}$ CUPS RICE

1 CUP SHREDDED SWEET POTATO

1 CUP BROCCOLI FLORETS

$\frac{1}{4}$ TEASPOON BLACK PEPPER

$\frac{1}{4}$ CUP SHREDDED LOW-FAT CHEDDAR CHEESE

1. Heat vegetable oil in large saucepan.
2. Add onions and mushrooms and cook on medium heat for 5 minutes.
3. Add broth, rice, sweet potato, broccoli, and pepper.
4. Bring to a boil, reduce heat, cover, and simmer for 20 minutes.
5. Place mixture in a greased 2-quart casserole dish and sprinkle with cheese.
6. Broil until cheese melts.

Serves 6.

Hanukkah

MIRACLE OF LIGHTS

"JUDAH AND HIS BROTHERS WITH ALL OF ISRAEL ORDAINED THAT THE DAYS OF THE
DEDICATION OF THE ALTAR SHOULD BE KEPT IN THEIR SEASON FROM YEAR TO YEAR
FOR EIGHT DAYS . . . WITH MIRTH AND GLADNESS."

Apocrypha: Maccabees 1:1

ONE QUIET MORNING, a band of rough-looking soldiers came to
Modin, a little village in the northern kingdom of Israel. They had been
sent there by the wicked king Antiochus of Syria.

Antiochus had greatly hurt the Jewish people. He had seized their
holy and very beautiful Temple in Jerusalem. He had befouled it with
pigs and with statues of Syrian gods. And he had put out the Temple's
ever-burning light, a symbol of God's love.

Now the people of Modin feared what Antiochus might do next.
Would he forbid them to keep the Sabbath? Would he keep them from
praying to God in their own way?

A crowd slowly gathered in the village square. There was a loud
murmur as they huddled together.

The tall Syrian captain strode to the center of the square. He was
dressed in heavy armor. A pointed silver helmet covered his head. In his
hand he held a wide, shining sword.

"Listen, Jews," the captain commanded. "King Antiochus has

conquered your land. Judea now belongs to him. From now on, you must worship Syrian gods. Anyone resisting will be put to death!"

At once, some soldiers brought out a giant gold statue. Soon it stood gleaming in the heart of the town.

"Each of you must bow down to this statue," the captain barked at the villagers. "He is a great Syrian god."

Mattathias, an elderly Jewish priest, stood off to the side. His five sons surrounded him. Although eighty years old, Mattathias was still tall and upright. All the villagers respected him for his wisdom and courage.

"If a man calls a statue god, does that make it God?" Mattathias called out. His voice sounded strong and forceful.

A hush fell over the crowd. The captain pointed to Mattathias and said, "You are a Jewish priest. You must be first. Bow down to our statue."

Mattathias turned away. He followed only the laws of his people. And he believed in only one God. Let the whole world comply with the king's wishes. Mattathias knew that he and his sons would not.

The enraged captain approached the old man. "Obey the king, or we will hang you," he threatened.

Mattathias wheeled around. He looked right into the officer's eyes. Then he spoke sharply for all to hear, "I will *never* break my bond with God. I will *never* bow down to a statue. I will *never* stop being a Jew."

None of the other Jews spoke. Few were as brave as Mattathias.

Some minutes went by. Finally a timid shopkeeper stepped forward. He smiled weakly at the soldiers. "Mattathias will not obey the king," he said. "But I will." And he kneeled before the figure.

Mattathias strode forward. He raised his clenched fist. With one hard blow, he knocked the shopkeeper over. The man landed on his back.

Many villagers shuddered in fear. "What will happen now?" a daughter whispered to her mother.

With alarm, they watched Mattathias pull a knife from his belt and lunge at the Syrian leader. The captain fell dead. Then Mattathias pushed over the statue. It smashed to bits.

For moments, everyone stood silent. Mattathias then lifted his arms high into the air. He cried out, "*Mi Ladonai Elai*, Whoever is for God's law, follow me." With that, Mattathias and his sons turned and fled. They headed for the hills. A handful of men and boys followed close behind.

The Syrians pursued the Jews on horseback and on foot. They followed them as far as the hilly slopes. But they could not catch up to them. Discouraged, they returned to camp to regroup their forces.

The outlaws were now high above the village. They hid in caves. Only when darkness fell did Mattathias and the others crawl out of their hiding places. Far off they could see Jerusalem, the holy city.

"One day we will overcome our Syrian foes," the would-be fighters vowed. "We will go to Jerusalem. We will take back our Temple. And we'll free the city from the infidels."

Many days passed. Eventually Mattathias took sick and died. But before he died, he blessed his son Judah. Mattathias asked all those who had followed him to now follow Judah, the bravest of all the sons.

Gradually more Jews joined the struggle against the Syrians. The newcomers came prepared to fight. They arrived from every part of the land. Some carried baskets of fruit, pretending they were going to the market. Others dressed like shepherds, and came driving herds of animals. But under their robes, all bore swords, clubs, bows, and arrows.

The months stretched on. But Judah and his men were not idle. From their hiding places, the Jewish fighters spied on the powerful Syrian forces. Though few in number, the Jews tormented their foes with daily sneak attacks. Often, they stole into the enemy's camps and struck hard with their crude weapons. Judah's every blow was so deadly that people began to call him the Maccabee, which means the "hammer." Soon his followers became known as the Maccabees.

Three years passed. Judah's army was still small. And the Syrian army was very big. Yet the Maccabees were unafraid. At last they felt ready to wage all-out war against their enemies.

On the night of the first big battle, Judah addressed his men. "We will defeat the wicked Antiochus," he boldly promised. "We will drive him from our land. It's time to take back our holy Temple in Jerusalem."

When darkness fell, the Maccabees crept noiselessly down from their hiding places in the mountains. With swords and flames, they surprised the Syrian soldiers where they lay sleeping. Suddenly awakened, the Syrians staggered out of their burning tents. Many tried to escape. But Judah and his men pursued them. They killed thousands of Syrian soldiers. The rest scattered and ran away.

News of the defeat soon reached King Antiochus. He was enraged. "Let us send a larger force to crush the Maccabees," the king ordered.

"How can so few of us fight against so many?" Judah's men worried.

"Be not afraid," Judah told them. "If victory goes only to the bigger army, we would indeed be lost. But we fight for our God. With the strength that God gives us, we will win!"

Judah's brave words cheered his followers. They prepared a new attack. The men sounded their trumpets. Then, with loud shouts and songs of praise to God, they stormed down from the hilltops and into the second great battle. The small band of Jews swept forward and struck down many Syrian soldiers. They destroyed camp after camp. Soon nothing was left of the powerful Syrian force.

Antiochus was in a rage. "Order a *third* army into battle!" he thundered. Forty thousand foot soldiers and seven thousand cavalry readied themselves to attack Judah and his men. Helmets glittering and horses clattering, the huge army advanced on the small band of Jews.

Judah acted quickly. He ordered his forces to flee into the forest. When the Syrians arrived, they found no one there.

The troops were confused and bewildered. They plunged into the woods to look for the Maccabees. But after three years of living in the mountains, the Maccabees knew every tree and bush. They easily trapped and overcame the Syrian soldiers. The Syrians tried to flee. But wherever they turned, the Maccabees stood waiting for them. Judah destroyed Antiochus's third army. The battle for religious freedom was won. At long last, the war was over.

Judah rallied his weary troops. "We were an army small in number. But together we crushed our mighty invaders. Our land of Judea is free again. Now let us reclaim Jerusalem, the gateway to Heaven, and our holy Temple." Judah and his army set forth for Jerusalem. Singing loudly of their victory, the soldiers marched to the sacred city.

But as they passed through the gates of the city, their voices grew still. Jerusalem was in ruins! The buildings stood smashed and empty. Weeds and grass grew in the deserted streets. Wild animals ran about. There was filth and dirt everywhere. The air was deathly quiet.

In front of many homes stood low, carved stone tables. "I know these tables," muttered one of Judah's men. "They are Syrian altars. On them Syrians forced us to make sacrifices to their gods."

Sadly the soldiers walked on. Presently they reached the Temple, the center of Jewish holiness. The men gasped. The mighty gates were burned. The walls were crumbling. Almost everything was either damaged or destroyed. Even the inner courts were strewn with garbage and overgrown with weeds. But most shocking of all was the altar. The soldiers wept at the horrible sight. "Almighty God, protect Thy people Israel," someone prayed quietly. "A Syrian idol sits there!"

Without a word, Judah and his men approached the blessed place. They took hold of the heavy gold statue and carried it out. Beyond the Temple gates, they tossed it down. It smashed into many pieces. Then the soldiers went back into the Temple. "How shall we cleanse the altar?" Judah asked. "Its sacred stones are covered with the blood of hogs."

"Let us take apart the altar, stone by stone," the High Priest replied. "We'll put the stones aside. Then Jewish hands can build a new altar."

Feverishly the Jews worked. They rebuilt the altar. They repaired the walls, doors, and courts. They swept and scrubbed the Temple floors. They molded new holy vessels and burned sweet-smelling spices. They decorated the Temple front with golden crowns and shields.

Finally, all was ready. It was time to celebrate the return to the Temple. "When shall the festival start?" a shepherd in Judah's army asked.

A silence fell. Then the High Priest said, "The twenty-fifth of Kislev is but a few days off. It is the depth of winter, a time of short days and much darkness. We have always marked that day with song and prayers. Why not rededicate the Temple to the service of God on that day?"

"A happy idea," everyone agreed.

The evening of the celebration arrived. The High Priest was getting ready. He asked someone to bring holy oil to light the sacred lamp.

But there was no holy oil to be found anywhere.

Suddenly someone found a very small jar of pure oil. The High Priest looked at it closely. "Thanks be to God," he said. "The seal is not broken. The oil is still holy."

"But there is no use lighting it," a soldier cried. "There is so little oil. It will only last one day."

"We must have faith," said the High Priest.

So the High Priest broke the seal. He poured the oil into the lamp and lit it. The light burned all that day and all that night. It burned the next day. And the next. And the next. No one could believe it. The lamp burned for eight days!

"A miracle!" the people cried. "A great wonder has happened here."

For eight days, the Jews offered prayers of thanksgiving. They waved branches of palm. They danced. They praised God with song and with harps and cymbals. The hills of Judea echoed with their happy melodies.

The High Priest spoke to the people. He told them to celebrate Hanukkah, the dedication of the Temple in Jerusalem, each year. "For eight days, you shall be glad and joyful," he said. "And on each evening, you are to light lamps on the doors of the houses. The lights are to serve as signs of the great miracle of life."

The basic story can be found in the Apocrypha, semi-sacred writings that are not part of the Bible. Maccabees, Book 1, Chapters 1 through 4, and the Babylonian Talmud are the chief sources.

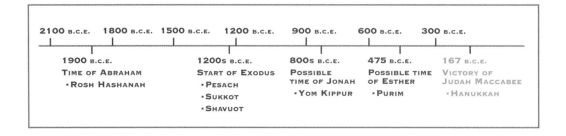

WHAT WE CELEBRATE

IN ANCIENT TIMES, the Jews had a yearly midwinter celebration. It marked the time of year when days are shortest, just before they begin to grow longer. The holiday was a festival of joy and was observed as a second Sukkot.

Much later in Jewish history, in the winter of 167 B.C.E., Judah and his followers triumphed over the Syrians and rededicated the Temple. Jews decided to add the victory and the rededication to the seasonal holiday. They named the celebration Hanukkah, the Hebrew word for "dedication."

No one is entirely sure where the name Maccabees came from. Some people think that the fighters took the name from the Hebrew word for "hammer," *makkeb*. But others say that Judah's battle flag displayed the letters M-K-B-Y. They stood for the words *Mi Chamocha Ba-elim Yhvh*, Hebrew for, "Who is like unto Thee among the gods, O Lord?" In either case, the heroes who freed their people from religious persecution came to be called Maccabees.

Today, Jews celebrate Hanukkah as a reminder of the wondrous miracles that occurred long ago. It is a miracle that the faith and courage of a few Jews were able to overcome the might and power of many Syrians. It is a miracle that the little cruse of oil in the Temple burned for eight days. It is a miracle that the Jews survived thousands of years of oppression in many different lands.

Though tiny in number, Mattathias and his sons were ready to lay down their lives for the right to worship. With that faith, they were able to crush a host of enemies and establish the idea of religious freedom that we enjoy today.

HOW WE CELEBRATE

THE MOST IMPORTANT SYMBOL of Hanukkah is the eight-branched *hanukkiah*, which is a kind of *menorah*, or "candelabrum." The first candle is lit on the eve of the twenty-fifth day of Kislev, which falls in November or December. The person kindling the candle puts it into the farthest hole on the right of the menorah and adds an additional candle each night to show the importance of each new day of Hanukkah. The candles are lit from left to right. A special additional candle, the *shammash*, kindles the other candles.

The nightly increase in light anticipates longer days as winter gives way to spring. But the growing radiance has other meanings, too. It shows that full freedom is achieved only in stages. And, just as the light from the burning oil cast a glow of freedom on the Jewish people, each belief, or "light," no matter how small, can continue and grow without limit.

Of course, Hanukkah has also become a time of gift giving. In some families, the children get a small present on each of the eight evenings of the holiday. A favorite gift is Hanukkah *gelt*, the Yiddish word for "money." Sometimes this takes the form of sweet chocolate shaped like coins and wrapped in gold or silver foil.

Jews eat foods containing cheese at Hanukkah to honor a woman named Judith whose bravery helped win the war over the Syrians. Judith was a pious woman who learned that the Syrians were about to kill all the Jews in her town. To save her people, Judith pretended to be a traitor. She offered to tell Holofernes, a Syrian leader, how to defeat the Jews. To win his trust, Judith fed him cheese and wine. The cheese made Holofernes very thirsty. So he drank wine. The wine made him drunk. When Holofernes passed out, Judith beheaded him. She brought his head back home and had it placed on the city gates. Later the attacking Syrians saw their leader's head. Frightened, they ran away, sparing the Jews further warfare.

At first, people celebrated Hanukkah by making pancakes with cheese. Later, eating pancakes of all kinds became the custom. Potato pancakes, called *latkes* in Yiddish, are a great favorite. So, too, are *sufganiyot*, or jelly doughnuts, that have long been eaten by Sephardic Jews and are very popular in Israel. Foods made with oil or other fats symbolize the miracle of the oil found in the Temple.

CRAFTS AND FOOD

HOMEMADE MENORAHS
Here are two simple-to-make Hanukkah menorahs.

CLAY MENORAH • *All ages.*
YOU'LL NEED:

    CLAY

    HANUKKAH CANDLES

1. Form some clay into a bar about 10 inches long, 2 inches wide, and 2 inches thick.

2. Add more clay to 1 end to make it 3 inches thick. The thicker end is for the shammash, the candle you will use to light the others.

3. Use the bottom of 1 of your Hanukkah candles to poke 8 holes along the bar and a ninth hole in the thicker part for the shammash.

PAPER CUP MENORAH • *All ages.*

YOU'LL NEED:

10 SMALL PAPER CUPS

SAND

HANUKKAH CANDLES

METAL TRAY

1. Glue bottom of 1 cup to bottom of another to make a taller holder for the shammash.

2. Fill 8 single cups and the top of the double cup with sand.

3. Place cups in a row on a metal tray.

4. Light an additional candle on each night of Hanukkah, with the shammash in the top of the double cup.

HOMEMADE DREIDELS

By far the most popular Hanukkah game is Spin the Dreidel. A *dreidel*, Yiddish for a four-sided spinning top, has a Hebrew letter on each side. The four Hebrew letters, *Nun* (נ), *Gimel* (ג), *Hey* (ה), and *Shin* (ש), appear on the four sides. The letters are believed to be an acrostic of the sentence, "*Nes Gadol Hayah Sham*, A great miracle happened there." Here are two easy ways to make your own dreidel as well as directions for playing the game.

EGG CARTON DREIDEL • *All ages — with adult help.*

YOU'LL NEED:

CARDBOARD EGG CARTON

SCISSORS

SHORT PENCIL

1. Carefully cut 1 cup from the bottom of the egg carton. Use scissors to notch 4 equidistant points around top of cup.
2. Mark points with the 4 Hebrew letters: נ, ג, ה, ש.
3. Push a short, sharp pencil through the center of the cup.
4. Hold top of pencil to spin the dreidel.

CLAY DREIDEL • *All ages.*

YOU'LL NEED:

CLAY THAT DRIES HARD

PENCIL

1. Form a cube out of the clay.
2. Use pencil to carve the Hebrew letters (נ, ג, ה, ש), 1 on each side.
3. With extra clay, form a point at the bottom and a spinner at the top.
4. Let dry.

SPIN THE DREIDEL DIRECTIONS

Any number of people can play Spin the Dreidel. To start, everyone puts a penny in the pot, or center of the table. (You can also play with nuts, raisins, or candy.) The first player spins the dreidel and waits for it to fall. The side facing up when it falls tells the player what to do:

נ N (*Nun* or *nisht*) means you don't win or lose any pennies.

ג G (*Gimel* or *ganz*) means you get all the money.

ה H (*Hey* or *halb*) means you get half the money in the pot.

ש Sh (*Shin* or *shtel*) means you put in one penny.

After each player's turn, everyone puts another penny in the pot. You can play as many rounds as you like. The one who has the most pennies at the end wins.

LATKES • *Ages 8 and up — with adult help.*

YOU'LL NEED:

PAPER TOWELS	LARGE FRYING PAN
PEELER	4 LARGE POTATOES
GRATER	3 TABLESPOONS MATZAH MEAL
COLANDER	3 EGGS, BEATEN
MIXING BOWL	1 TEASPOON SALT
WOODEN MIXING SPOON	$\frac{1}{4}$ TEASPOON PEPPER
MEASURING SPOONS	OIL FOR FRYING
	APPLESAUCE

1. Peel and grate potatoes.

2. Drain off any water in a colander.

3. Place grated potatoes into mixing bowl and add matzah meal, eggs, salt, and pepper. Mix well.

4. Heat 1 to 2 tablespoons of oil in large frying pan. Drop in 1 large spoonful of mixture for each latke. Fry a few latkes at a time for 2 minutes on each side until brown. Add more oil as needed.

5. Drain on paper towels and serve with applesauce.

Serves 6.

SUFGANIYOT (JELLY DOUGHNUTS)

Ages 8 and up — with adult help.

YOU'LL NEED:

ROUND COOKIE CUTTER	4 TABLESPOONS DRY YEAST
LARGE BOWL	1/4 CUP WARM WATER
WOODEN MIXING SPOON	2 TABLESPOONS SUGAR
CLEAN, DAMP TOWEL	3 EGG YOLKS
LIGHTLY FLOURED BOARD	3/4 CUP WARM MILK
MEASURING CUP AND SPOONS	3 1/2 CUPS FLOUR
LARGE SAUCEPAN	PLUM OR STRAWBERRY JAM
SLOTTED SPOON	OIL FOR FRYING
PAPER TOWELS	POWDERED SUGAR

1. Dissolve yeast in warm water.

2. Add sugar and stir until bubbly.

3. Beat in egg yolks.

4. Add 3 cups flour and 3/4 cup warm milk slowly. Stir until dough forms a ball.

5. Place dough on a lightly floured board.

6. Knead for about 10 minutes until dough does not stick to board or hand.

7. Place dough back in bowl and cover with clean, damp towel.

8. Let dough rise for about 2 hours, or until it doubles in size.

9. Put dough back on lightly floured board. Punch down and roll out until it is about 1/4 inch thick.

10. Cut circles of dough. (If you don't have a cookie cutter, use the rim of a drinking glass to cut round shapes.)

11. On 1 circle place a teaspoon of jam. Cover with another circle and pinch edges together.

12. Repeat step 11 until all circles are used up.

13. Place about 3 inches of oil in large saucepan.

14. Heat oil and fry a few doughnuts at a time until golden.

15. Remove with a slotted spoon and drain on paper towels.

16. Roll warm doughnuts in powdered sugar.

Makes about 18 sufganiyot.

Purim

QUEEN ESTHER SAVES HER PEOPLE

"AND MORDECAI SENT LETTERS UNTO ALL THE JEWS . . .

TO ENJOIN THEM TO KEEP THE FOURTEENTH AND FIFTEENTH DAYS OF ADAR,

YEARLY . . . TO MAKE THEM DAYS OF FEASTING AND GLADNESS,

AND OF SENDING PORTIONS ONE TO ANOTHER, AND GIFTS TO THE POOR."

Book of Esther 9:20–22

IN THE SIXTH CENTURY, B.C.E., many Jews left Judea and settled in Babylon and other parts of Persia. They lived there in peace until King Ahasuerus ascended the throne. His reign was the beginning of sad days for the Jews of the kingdom.

One day the powerful King Ahasuerus gave a huge feast in his palace. Wanting to show off his great wealth, he bellowed, "Give my guests the finest wine in vessels of gold. Let them enjoy my generosity."

The feast went on and on. By the seventh day, the king was very merry from all the wine he had been drinking. Rashly he called his servants into the room. "Bring Vashti the queen before me," he told them. "Let all see how beautiful she is."

The servants went to fetch the queen. But they returned without her. "She will not come, Your Majesty," they told him, bowing low.

"How *dare* she defy me!" the vain king shouted, climbing down from his throne. His face was red with rage.

Angrily he paced back and forth. Then the king climbed back onto his throne. Turning to his advisers, he asked impulsively, "What shall be done with a queen who does not obey her king?"

"She must be sent away," his courtiers advised. "And the king should choose a new maiden to be queen."

King Ahasuerus was not sure he liked the idea. But he didn't want to appear weak before the court. So he agreed. Then he asked his wise men, "How will we choose someone new?"

"Gather into your palace all the fair young women of the kingdom," they suggested. "Meet each in turn. Let the most pleasing one become your queen."

The king hesitated, but then agreed. He sent for his soldiers. "Mount your horses," he ordered. "Speedily bring me the most beautiful maidens in the kingdom."

The king's men traveled throughout the land. After many days, they came to the home of a Jew named Mordecai.

"The king is choosing a new queen," they announced. "All beautiful young women must be brought to the palace. Is there a maiden living within?"

Mordecai thought of the gentle Esther, who lived with him. She was his uncle's daughter. After her parents died, Mordecai took her in and cared for her as if she were his own child.

Mordecai asked the horsemen to wait. He went to speak with Esther. The girl had never looked more lovely. Her dark hair hung down in two heavy, long braids. Her deep brown eyes shone bright with intelligence and gaiety.

"My dear child," Mordecai said, "the king is seeking a new queen. Perhaps he will favor you. You are so lovely to look at."

Esther remained calm. "But, Cousin, I have no desire to live in the palace," she said quietly. "I would much rather live here with you. Besides, I am a Jew. I want to remain among Jews."

Mordecai found it hard to continue. But he felt he had to speak. "It is important that you do as I ask," he said. "Go live in the palace. But do not tell anyone that you are a Jew. Who knows? One day you may be able to help your people."

So it was. Esther decided to do as Mordecai asked. She went to the king's palace. When she arrived many young women from around the land were already there.

Each day, a guard chose one woman to appear before the king. Slaves dressed the maiden in rich clothes and doused her with heavy perfumes. Then she entered the throne room and passed before the king and his court.

The king studied each new woman in turn. They were all very beautiful. But in every woman he found some fault. With a wave, he sent her away.

At last, the king summoned Esther to his chamber. The pretty young woman insisted on dressing herself. She wore simple clothes and no jewels. "I will present myself to the king as I am," she said. Head held high, she walked toward the throne.

The king gazed on her natural beauty and was very pleased. He loved her poise and stately carriage.

After a few minutes he descended his throne slowly and took her hand. "My dear," he said. "You are more wondrous than all the others together. You are the maiden whom I shall make my queen."

Esther cast down her stunning brown eyes. To the king, she said nothing. But to herself she thought, I must never forget who I am. One day I may be able to help my people.

A few days later, King Ahasuerus crowned Esther queen. She sat beside him. He held a great feast in her honor.

From then on, Mordecai would often come to the courtyard of the palace to see Esther. They talked and exchanged news. But she never told anyone that he was her cousin.

One day, Mordecai came to the palace courtyard as usual. But this time, he had something very important to tell Esther. He whispered the message in her ear. "I have overheard two officers talking. They are planning to kill the king. Tell him at once of the plot. Warn him to beware."

Esther was shocked. She thought a moment and then said, "But I cannot go to the king without being summoned. He has forbidden it."

"You must go," urged her cousin. "Do not tremble. Give him my message."

The king was in his chamber. He was surprised to see the queen enter without being called. But he trusted Esther and listened gravely to her news. Stunned, the king gathered his nobles and sent them to investigate.

In a while they were back. "Mordecai has spoken the truth," they told the king. "There is such a plot!"

The king sprang to his feet. "Make haste," he shouted. "Capture the traitors!"

The men hurried off to do the king's bidding. By nightfall, they had caught and executed the conspirators.

Before he went to bed, the king called for his scribe. "Bring me the Book of Chronicles," he demanded. "I want you to record how Mordecai, the Jew, saved my life." The scribe came and wrote down the whole story.

Meanwhile, the king had an adviser in his court named Haman. He was a very wicked nobleman. Next to the king, Haman was the most powerful man in Persia. So high was his rank that the king had ordered everyone to bow down before him.

Early one morning, Haman was on his way to see the king. As Haman passed through the palace courtyard, he met Mordecai. To Haman's surprise, Mordecai did not bow down.

"Halt!" shouted Haman. "Kneel before me as the king has commanded."

"I will not," Mordecai answered boldly, "for I am a Jew. I bow before no one but God."

Haman seethed with anger. His face grew red. But he did nothing. Instead, he rushed off and told his head officer what Mordecai had said. The officer became just as enraged as Haman.

"Why do you not have him killed?" the officer asked. "In fact, why not get the king to kill all the Jews?"

The idea appealed to the evil Haman. In fact, the more he thought about it, the more he liked it. But he decided to think it over and come up with a clear plan of action.

That night, the king went to his bedchamber. But he could not sleep. To help pass the time, he called for his scribe.

"Read to me from the Book of Chronicles," the ruler asked, and the scribe started the narration. Soon, he came to the part that told how Mordecai had saved the king's life.

The king interrupted the reading. "That Jew, Mordecai," he asked. "Was he ever rewarded?"

"No, Your Majesty," the scribe answered. "He received nothing."

"Send for Haman early tomorrow," said the king. "We must honor Mordecai without delay."

Then the king dismissed the scribe, and for the rest of the night he tossed and turned on his couch.

Haman arrived at dawn the next day. "Show him in," the king called. Haman entered.

"What should be done for a man the king wants to honor?" Ahasuerus asked.

Haman beamed happily. He thought that the king meant him. So he said, "Dress that man in kingly robes. Seat him on your white horse. And let a noble prince lead him on horseback through the city saying, 'This is what we do to the man whom the king wishes to honor.'"

"Excellent!" cried the king. "Go quickly. Mordecai is the man. And you, Haman, shall lead the horse."

Haman trembled with rage. But he hid his true feelings from the king. Solemnly he carried out his order.

Haman set Mordecai on the horse, and led him through the streets. All the people praised and applauded the noble Jew as he passed by.

After that, Haman was more incensed than ever. His hatred of Mordecai and the Jews knew no bounds. Haman hurried to see the king. Under his arm, he carried his cruel plan to kill the Jews.

"Your Honor," Haman began, "there are people in this land who disobey Your Lordship."

"Who are these people?" mumbled the king. He was too busy enjoying his wine to look up.

"The Jews," said Haman. "If it pleases you, sir, these people should be punished. They do not follow your laws. They worship their own God."

The king finished the glass of wine. "What shall be done with them?" he asked calmly.

"They should be killed," said Haman.

"Killed?" asked the king sleepily. "When?"

"I have drawn lots to choose the date," Haman volunteered. "It is the thirteenth day of next month."

The king called for more wine. While he drank, Haman thrust the paper into the king's hand. "Place your royal seal on this decree, sir. And I will carry out your order."

The king took the paper but was too dizzy to read it. Slyly Haman urged him on. "Stamp it, sir. And I will put all the money I take from the Jews into your treasury."

"Very well," replied Ahasuerus, putting his mark on the document.

Soon the king's messengers set off on horseback. The riders carried the news to all the provinces of the kingdom.

At last, the horsemen reached Mordecai. Slowly he read the order to kill all Jews. A loud wail escaped his lips. "It must not be," he cried.

Mordecai went into his house. He dressed himself for mourning. He put on clothes of coarse sackcloth and scattered ashes on his head. Then he went and sat in the courtyard of the palace.

Presently Queen Esther appeared. She hurried over.

"What has happened?" she asked nervously. "You look so terribly sad."

"I fear the death of our people," Mordecai said. And he told her of the harsh ruling.

Esther paled. "What can I do?" she asked.

"Go to the king," Mordecai told her. "He loves you. Tell him that you are a Jew. And say that if the Jews die, you, too, will die."

"I cannot go again without being asked," Esther said. "Surely this time he will have me killed."

"Think not only of yourself, Esther," said Mordecai. "Think of your people."

Esther considered carefully what Mordecai had said. Finally she replied bravely, "I will do as you say. I will try to save my people."

She started to leave, but turned back. "I ask but one kindness," she said. "Have our people spend three days in prayer and fasting. My maids and I will also fast. Then I will be ready. Thus may I find favor in the eyes of the king. If I die, I die."

On the third day, Esther put on her crown and royal robes. Unafraid, she entered the throne room. There sat Ahasuerus, gold scepter in hand. At his side stood Haman.

Esther waited. Finally the king pointed his scepter. This showed that he was pleased to see her. She drew near.

The king noticed her eyes filled with dark shadows. Puzzled, he asked, "Why have you risked your life to come here? I have not called for you."

"Tomorrow I am giving a feast," she said. "I would like you to attend."

The king brightened. "I will be there," he answered.

Turning to Haman, she said, "You, too. Please come." The horrible man accepted with a bow. Then Esther turned and left the chamber.

The next day, Ahasuerus and Haman came to Esther's feast. She plied her guests with food and wine. The king was in a very jolly mood. He said to his wife, "Ask anything of me, my dear. It shall be yours."

"I ask only for my life," said Esther.

"What?" cried the king. "Your life? Who in this kingdom wishes you harm?"

"This man!" said Esther, pointing to Haman.

"I?" cried Haman, horrified.

Esther turned to the king. "Your Royal Highness has sealed an important decree. It states that all Jews be killed," said Esther.

"Well, what has that to do with you, my dear?" the king chortled.

"I am a Jew," said Esther. "If they perish, so do I."

The king dropped into a chair. "I did not know," he gasped.

"And you remember the Jew Mordecai," Esther went on, "who saved your life. He is my cousin."

The king had to calm himself. Slowly he arose and gazed out the window. There he saw the newly set-up gallows.

"Why the gallows?" the king asked Haman.

"I had them built for Mordecai," Haman replied.

"Then we'll hang *you* instead!" the king cried out.

The proud Haman fell to his knees. He begged for forgiveness. But the king called his guards. They dragged Haman to the gallows and hanged him.

Esther still looked unhappy and forlorn. "What will become of my people?" she pleaded.

"The decree must stand," said the king sadly. "It is the law of the land."

"Then send out another decree," Esther said. "Let it say that the Jews may defend themselves if attacked."

"So shall it be," said the king.

The fateful day arrived. The Persian enemies rose up against the Jews. But the Jews joined together and fought back. With sword and club, they drove off their attackers.

Messengers brought the king news of the Jews' victory. The king sent for Mordecai. "Your people are very brave," the king said. "And you are a wise man. I wish you to take Haman's place in my court."

The word quickly spread throughout the kingdom. Haman's plot had failed. Queen Esther had saved her people. Justice had triumphed over evil. And the fourteenth day of Adar became a day of rejoicing instead of a day of grief for Jews everywhere.

The basic story was adapted from the Bible, Book of Esther, Chapters 1 through 10. On Purim, the Book of Esther is read from a scroll called the Megillah.

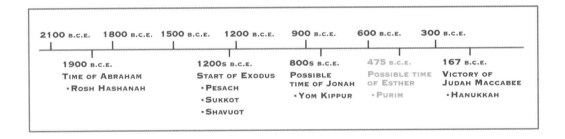

WHAT WE CELEBRATE

LONG, LONG AGO, the day on which Jews celebrate Purim, the fourteenth day of Adar, was a nature festival. Linked to the passing of winter and the approach of spring, the day was celebrated with joy and revelry — as indeed it still is.

Today the Feast of Purim usually begins sometime in February or March. The holiday commemorates the deliverance of the Jews of Persia from the wicked Haman. Its Hebrew name, Purim, has come to mean "Feast of Lots." The name comes from the Persian word *pur*, for "lot," the game of chance that Haman used to decide on which day to kill the Jews.

Purim is also a time to recall the escape of the Jewish people from past persecution, from earliest times to the present. Hundreds of Jewish communities and families all over the world celebrate their own special Purim. A group in Prague, for example, remembers a rabbi who was saved from a death sentence in 1629, while Jews in Portugal celebrate their triumph over danger in 1578.

Most scholars agree that the story of Esther is very old, and not based on historical fact. But to Jews, it remains ever new. The story reminds them of other Hamans, past and in recent times, who have tried to destroy the Jewish people.

The Book of Esther never mentions the name of God. Nevertheless, the story suggests that God works in mysterious ways. It celebrates Esther's faith and determination in the face of danger. And it makes clear that Jews must struggle against the enemies that seek to destroy them. A good number of Jews fast on the day before Purim, the thirteenth of Adar. It is called the Fast of Esther, and it notes Esther's bravery in delivering her people from harm.

HOW WE CELEBRATE

THE BOOK OF ESTHER is part of the Bible called The Writings. It tells Jews to celebrate the deliverance of the Jews of Persia with "days of feasting and gladness." People eat festive meals in the late afternoon and nibble special treats. These include the three-cornered *hamantaschen*, which represent the three-cornered hat Haman wore when he served Ahasuerus.

The Book of Esther also tells people to "send portions one to another." Thus, friends and neighbors exchange food gifts of hamantaschen, fruit, and cookies. These gifts are called *shalach manot* in Hebrew, and *schlach monos* in Yiddish.

Gifts to the poor is another obligation on Purim. The tradition is to give money, food, or clothes to at least two needy people. Especially during the holiday, Jews are expected to care for any poor person who asks for help.

At services on the eve of Purim and again in the morning, the Book of Esther is read from a handwritten scroll called the *Megillah*. The *Megillah* says of Haman, "May his name be erased." So listeners make a lot of noise each time they hear the name Haman. Some shake groggers or rattles, while others stamp their feet noisily to drown out the name.

On Purim, it is also usual to dress up in masks and costumes, and become characters in the Book of Esther. Both making noise and dressing up were originally ways of protecting oneself against evil spirits at the change of seasons. Many communities traditionally perform Purim *schpiels*, Yiddish for "plays." Some say that people dress up, appearing different from who they really are, to show that the divine spirit is puzzling and things often are not what they seem to be.

Purim, then, is a time to feel good, to have fun, and to be someone other than yourself. According to Jewish tradition, each person on Purim should be so joyful as "not to know" (*ad lo yada* in Hebrew) the difference between "blessed Mordecai" and "cursed Haman." For this reason, in Israel the festive Purim carnival is called *Adloyada*.

CRAFTS AND FOOD

SIMPLE PURIM GROGGER • *All ages.*

Reading the *Megillah* is an important part of any Purim celebration. Shake the grogger every time Haman's name is mentioned.

YOU'LL NEED:

> EMPTY TIN CAN
>
> ALUMINUM FOIL
>
> UNCOOKED RICE, BEANS, OR SMALL PEBBLES
>
> PAPER
>
> TAPE
>
> PAINT OR CRAYONS
>
> RUBBER BANDS

1. Partly fill empty tin can with uncooked rice, beans, or small pebbles.
2. Make a lid of aluminum foil and secure with rubber bands.
3. Wrap paper around the entire can and tape to fit securely.
4. Decorate with paint or crayons.

PURIM PUPPET HEADS • *All ages — with adult help.*

Make your own papier-mâché puppets to dramatize the *Megillah*, and put on Purim schpiels at home for friends or family.

YOU'LL NEED:

> NEWSPAPER
>
> MASKING TAPE
>
> TUBE FROM PAPER TOWELS OR TOILET PAPER
>
> LARGE EMPTY SODA BOTTLE

1 CUP FLOUR

1 CUP WATER

MIXING BOWL

PAPER TOWELS

TEMPERA PAINT

GLUE

SCRAP CLOTH

1. For puppet's face, crumple 2 sheets of newspaper into a softball-sized ball.

2. Wrap strips of masking tape around it to keep the shape.

3. Cut off 3 inches from the cardboard tube. Fit tube over soda bottle neck and attach with masking tape.

4. Attach newspaper ball to cardboard tube with masking tape.

5. Tear strips of newspaper and tape onto puppet to make thick braids for Esther, a beard for Mordecai, triangular ears for Haman, or other features.

6. Mix 1 cup flour and 1 cup water, and stir by hand until thick and smooth. This is the paste to mold the head and features.

7. Tear 10 sheets of paper towel into strips.

8. Dip 1 strip into paste. Squeeze off excess paste with 2 fingers and place strip over newspaper ball. Smooth and shape strip while still damp.

9. Repeat step 8 over and over until entire ball and features are covered. (Tear more strips, if necessary.)

10. Let puppet head dry overnight.

11. Paint head and face with tempera paint and let dry.

12. Glue a large piece of scrap cloth around top of cardboard tube, beneath base of head. Be sure cloth is large enough to cover your hand.

13. Remove tube from soda bottle, and insert your fingers into the tube to control the head.

Makes 1 puppet.

HAMANTASCHEN • *Ages 8 and up — with adult help.*

These triangular pastries are a favorite Purim food. You may also give them as gifts, or shalach manot, to friends.

YOU'LL NEED:

MIXING BOWL	4 CUPS FLOUR
ROLLING PIN	2 TEASPOONS BAKING POWDER
MEASURING CUP AND SPOONS	$^3/_4$ CUP SUGAR
ROUND COOKIE CUTTER	4 EGGS
LIGHTLY GREASED COOKIE SHEET	$^1/_3$ CUP WATER
	$^1/_3$ CUP OIL
	POPPYSEED, PRUNE, OR
	APRICOT PASTRY FILLING

1. Sift flour, baking powder, and sugar into mixing bowl.
2. Break eggs into center, add oil and water, and mix. Knead until smooth.
3. Form dough into a ball, and divide ball into 4 parts.
4. Roll out 1 part into a thin sheet and cut into 3-inch rounds. (If you don't have a cookie cutter, use the rim of a drinking glass to cut round shapes.)
5. Put a teaspoon of filling in center.
6. Draw up on 2 sides and then pull the third side across. Pinch edges together to form a 3-cornered pocket.
7. Repeat steps 4 through 6 until you've used up all the dough.
8. Preheat oven to 350 degrees Fahrenheit.
9. Bake on a lightly greased cookie sheet for about half an hour or until lightly browned.

Makes about 50 hamantaschen.

Pesach

LET MY PEOPLE GO

"The fourteenth day of the first month, at dusk is the Lord's Passover.
And on the fifteenth day of the same month is the feast
of unleavened bread; seven days you shall eat unleavened bread."

Leviticus 23:5–9

For many, many years, the descendants of Abraham lived happily in Canaan. Then something terrible happened. There was a severe famine. No grain grew. There was no bread to eat.

Some Israelites stayed and starved in Canaan. But others fled. They gathered their belongings and went down to Egypt. There they settled, tending their herds of sheep and cattle. For a long while, the Israelites grew in number and prospered.

Finally the time of plenty ended. A cruel and selfish pharaoh began to rule over Egypt. This pharaoh was like a god to the Egyptians.

"I love to build," he said. "The poor people of my land and my captives will be my slaves. They will glorify me by erecting monuments, temples, and palaces."

And so it was. Slaves put up building after building for the pharaoh. But he always wanted more. He dreamed of setting up whole new cities. "For this, I need extra workers," he said.

Suddenly the pharaoh remembered the Israelites who had come to Egypt from Canaan. He feared their numbers and their power. One day they might rise up against me, he thought. "I will make them my slaves," the pharaoh decided. "They shall make bricks for my buildings."

The pharaoh issued an order to his soldiers. "Gather together all the Israelite men and boys. Put them to work at hard labor."

Soon, the Israelites were toiling under the hot sun of Egypt. Cruel overseers forced them to turn straw and clay into bricks for the pharaoh's cities. Day after day, they sweated in the broiling heat, with little to eat or drink.

"We refuse to be slaves," the Israelites complained bitterly to their guards. "We are free people. We were our own masters in Canaan."

The pharaoh heard that the Israelites were unhappy. But he could not understand why. "I treat them no worse than I treat my other slaves," he said. "Why do they complain while the other slaves accept their lot?"

"They are lazy," said the head taskmaster.

"Then let's make them work harder," replied the pharaoh.

Year after year, the pharaoh forced the Israelites to sweat and toil terribly for him. In time, they began to forget that they had once been a free people. Even as they suffered, they stopped complaining.

Still, the pharaoh was worried. The Israelites continued to grow in number. The pharaoh called for the army commander. "Have every son born to the Israelites thrown into the Nile River," he commanded. "With fewer Israelites, I will feel safer."

Around this time, Yocheved, an Israelite woman, gave birth to a beautiful boy. For three months, she hid him from the pharaoh's soldiers. But then he became too big to hide.

Yocheved had an idea. "Let us make a basket for the baby," she told her daughter, Miriam. "We'll fill the cracks with tar so it will float."

"Then what?" asked Miriam.

Yocheved took a deep breath. "We'll put the basket among the reeds in the river. The pharaoh's daughter comes down to the river every day to bathe. Perhaps she will find the boy and care for him."

Miriam helped her mother prepare the basket. Carefully they placed the baby inside. Together they set it among the reeds in the river.

"You hide on the bank," Yocheved whispered to Miriam. "Watch what happens to the child." With that, she went away.

Miriam sat and waited. Presently she heard young women talking and laughing. It was the princess and her maidens.

"Look over there," said the princess. "I see something in the reeds."

"It looks like a basket," answered one of the maidens.

"Fetch it for me," the princess ordered.

The maid waded into the river and scooped up the basket. She brought it to the princess. On opening it, the princess saw the child. "Poor little baby," she said. "He must be one of the Israelite children."

The princess thought a moment. "I do not want him to die," she said aloud. "We must take him back to the palace."

"What will you do then, my lady?" her maid asked.

"I will raise him as my own son. He will be called Moses. That name means 'drawn out of the water.'"

"But the child will need a wet nurse," said the maid.

Miriam rushed out of her hiding place. "I know a nurse!" she shouted.

The princess was startled at first. But then she grew calm. After a few moments she spoke. "You may bring the nurse here," she told Miriam.

Miriam dashed off. Minutes later she returned with her mother.

"Nurse this child," the princess told Yocheved. "I will pay you well."

"Yes, indeed," said the woman, trying hard to hide her true feelings.

Yocheved took the child home and nursed him there until he was three years old. She told him that he was an Israelite. Again and again, she explained how his people had come to Egypt and become slaves.

"Soon you will go to live in the pharaoh's palace," Yocheved said. "But you must remember that you are an Israelite. Tell no one that you are descended from Abraham and Sarah. One day you may free your people and lead them back to Canaan."

Not long after, Moses moved into the palace. The princess treated him very well. She dressed him in rich robes. She gave him splendid horses to ride. Nevertheless, he remembered what his mother had said. And he dreamed of helping his people out of Egypt.

On a summer day, after he was grown-up, Moses was out walking. He stopped to watch some Israelite slaves at work. The men were stripped to their waists. They were carrying heavy loads of bricks. Moses saw an old Israelite stumble and fall. The man's pile of bricks toppled over. An Egyptian taskmaster rushed over. *Snap!* He cracked his whip on the man's back. *Snap, snap, snap!* Again and again, he beat the Israelite.

"Stop!" Moses shouted, springing forward. With one hand, he ripped the whip away from the guard. With the other, he struck him a powerful blow. The Egyptian fell to the ground — dead!

Moses was stunned. He dared not return to the palace. The pharaoh would surely hang him for taking the guard's life. That night, Moses fled.

The young man escaped into the wilderness. He wandered for many days. At long last, he came to the city of Midian, at the edge of the desert. There he settled. In time, he married and became a shepherd.

Many more years passed. The pharaoh of Egypt died and a new pharaoh came to power. But the Israelites remained in bondage.

Even though Moses was free, he could not forget his enslaved people in Egypt. The thought of his fellow Israelites being lashed by whips troubled him. What can I do for my people? he wondered. Am I the one to help free them?

Then, one day, Moses was tending his sheep in the desert. He had an awesome vision. It was a bush in flames. The flames roared all around. Yet the leaves and branches did not burn up!

Moses approached the burning bush. From the plant came a voice. "I am the God of thy ancestors, the God of Abraham and Sarah, the God of Isaac and Rebecca, and the God of Jacob, Leah, and Rachel," the voice cried. "I have seen the suffering of my people who are in Egypt. I have come to deliver them out of the land of the Egyptians."

Moses bowed low to the ground.

"Return to Egypt," God said. "Free your people from slavery. Lead them back to Canaan."

Moses was now eighty years old. He looked up. "But I am afraid," he pleaded. "What if I am not up to the task?"

"Worry not," God answered. "I will be with you."

Moses arose slowly. He readied himself to return to the land of Egypt. By now he felt proud. God had chosen him above all others to take the Israelites out of slavery.

Meanwhile, God also sent Aaron, the brother of Moses, into the desert. The brothers met and traveled together to Egypt.

When they arrived, Moses and Aaron went straightaway to the mighty Pharaoh. They told him that they had come in the name of God. "The word of God is, 'Let my people go,'" they said.

Pharaoh laughed. "Why should I listen to what you say? Your God means nothing to me. I will not let your people go."

Moses and Aaron pleaded with Pharaoh. But he only snickered.

What happened next alarmed Moses. Not only did Pharaoh not free the Israelites, but he worked them harder. He forced them to produce even more bricks. At the same time, he gave them less to eat.

Moses spoke to God. "Why did you send me to Pharaoh? Since then, things have grown much worse for the Israelites."

"Pharaoh is very hard-hearted," said God. "I must make him change his ways. I will lay a plague upon the land of Egypt. Then he will have to let our people go."

Moses awaited God's command. "Go to the riverbank and hold your staff over the water," God said. "The water will turn to blood."

Moses did as he was told. The water turned dark red. The fish died. The Egyptians had no water to drink. They begged Pharaoh to let the Israelites go. Finally Pharaoh agreed. "They can leave if the plague is removed," he promised Moses.

God lifted the plague. But at the last moment, Pharaoh changed his mind. He refused to free the Israelites.

God then called down another plague on Egypt. It was the plague of frogs. Frogs of every kind covered the fields and homes of Egypt.

"Tell your God to take away the plague of frogs," Pharaoh told Moses, "and I promise to let your people go."

God took away the frogs. But again Pharaoh went back on his word.

Now God called forth more plagues on Egypt. There were plagues of lice crawling on the skin, wild beasts roaring in the roadways, diseases that could not be cured, boils that covered the whole body, hail smashing down on the Egyptian houses, locusts eating the plants, and darkness blotting out the sun. Each time, Pharaoh swore to free the slaves if God would lift the plague. And each time God agreed and took the plague away. Yet, after every pardon, Pharaoh went back on his word.

Finally God told Moses, "I have brought nine plagues upon Egypt, and still the Israelites are enslaved. It is time for the most horrible plague of all. I will kill all the firstborn in Egypt, from the eldest son of Pharaoh to the firstborn of all the cattle. Then Pharaoh surely will let our people go. Tell the Israelites to ready themselves."

"What must they do?" asked Moses.

"Every family shall prepare a lamb for roasting. Have them smear the blood of the lamb on their doorposts. The blood shall mark the houses where they live. When I see the blood I will pass over them, sparing them the deadly plague, as I strike down the land of Egypt."

Moses and Aaron spoke God's words to the Israelites. The people bowed their heads and worshipped. Then they went away and did as God had commanded. That evening, Egypt suffered the last plague. Every Egyptian family lost its oldest son. But no harm came to the sons of Israel.

Pharaoh sent for Moses. His eyes were red from weeping. "My own son is dead. Take your people out of Egypt. QUICKLY!"

The Israelites rushed to gather their belongings. They were in such a hurry that they had no time to bake bread. Instead they packed up their unbaked dough before it could rise, and rushed away.

God sent a beautiful pillar of cloud to lead the people out of Egypt. At night it became a pillar of fire, like a torch. It helped them see where they were going, so they did not have to stop.

The Israelites marched by day and by night. Presently they reached the shores of the vast Red Sea. The sight made them terribly afraid. "How are we going to cross these deep waters? We have no boats!"

Moses looked around for some way to save them. Behind, in the distance, he saw Pharaoh's army. His horsemen and his chariots were coming swiftly after them. In front was the swirling seawater. It looked as though the Egyptians were going to overtake them.

Then Moses heard God's voice. "Raise your staff and hold it over the sea," God ordered.

Moses did so. The waters parted and became two towering walls. Between the walls there was a dry strip. Quickly the Israelites followed Moses between the waters to the other side.

When they reached the opposite shore, the people looked back. The soldiers of Pharaoh were rushing headlong between the walls of water. But all at once, the walls began to sway and tremble. With a thundering roar, the sea crashed down over the Egyptians. Horses, riders, and chariots all disappeared in the foaming water.

Safe on the far shore stood the Children of Israel. Happy that they were free at last, the people burst forth into song. They raised a magnificent cry. "We acknowledge God's great hand," they sang and shouted.

For seven days, they celebrated a festival for God who had brought them out of the land of Egypt. On each day, they ate only unleavened bread. No one worked, except in preparing the food. Then, with Moses in the lead, they began their long journey to the promised land of Canaan. So that they might never forget the birth of their freedom, the Israelites held a festival each year and called it Pesach, or Passover.

The basic story was adapted from the Bible, Book of Exodus, Chapters 1 through 14. The Passover story is read at the seder from a book called the Haggadah.

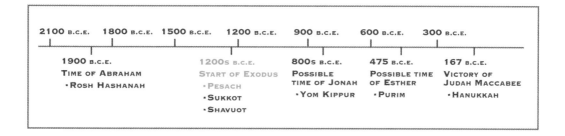

WHAT WE CELEBRATE

AFTER THE JEWS RETURNED TO CANAAN, they celebrated Pesach, Hebrew for "Passover," in the spring. That was when the lambs were sheared and the barley ripened in the fields. Families roasted whole lambs, which they ate together. Happy in their freedom, they retold the story of the Israelites in Egypt. After all, had Moses not heeded God and freed his people, there might not still be a Jewish people today.

At present, just as in ancient Canaan, Jews observe Passover as the Festival of Freedom. It commemorates the delivery of the Israelites from slavery, probably in the 1200s B.C.E. The name of the holiday comes from the last of the ten plagues that God visited on the Egyptians for keeping the Israelites in bondage. God killed the firstborn sons of the Egyptians but "passed over" the houses of the Israelites. The word also refers to the passing over of the Israelites from slavery to freedom.

The holiday begins on the eve of the fifteenth day of the month of Nisan, which falls in March or April. Some Jews celebrate for seven days and others observe eight days.

The Israelites did not have time to let their dough rise before they left Egypt. They took the dough with them and baked it in the heat of the desert sun. The result was flat, crisp, unleavened bread, which is called *matzah*, or *matzot* in its plural form. During Pesach, Jews eat matzah to remind them of the Exodus from Egypt. Another name for Pesach is *Chag ha-matzot*, which means "Festival of Unleavened Bread."

Matzah is also a symbol of people's faith in God. The Israelites were ordered to hurry from Egypt. They did not question the wisdom of going. They had complete trust that God would provide for them. Thus, the matzah symbolizes the hope that one day all Jews will have that same true faith.

Pesach started as a celebration of the coming of spring. Today its central meaning is freedom. In that way, the holiday of freedom and hope is also the holiday of spring and rebirth. Just as spring follows the bleakness of winter, so did freedom follow a life of slavery for the people of Israel. And just as the earth brings forth green life each spring, so did the Israelites begin a new life, journeying into the land of milk and honey.

HOW WE CELEBRATE

JEWS READY THEMSELVES FOR PESACH by cleaning their homes and removing all foods with leaven (any substance that causes fermentation). Special sets of dishes, pots, and pans take the place of everyday utensils. On the night before Pesach, it is the custom to search for hidden crumbs by candlelight and to use a feather to clean out the *chametz*, "leaven." For the rest of the holiday no leaven is eaten.

Traditionally, on the first night or first two nights of Pesach, Jews eat a ceremonial meal at home called the *seder*, which in Hebrew means "order." Instead of sitting upright in a chair, the leader usually reclines on pillows because that is how free people may sit.

On the table is the matzah, matzah cover, and a seder plate, with symbols that bring back the experiences of ancient days. The plate includes: *karpas* — greens, often parsley, that are dipped in salt water as a symbol of both spring and salty tears; *maror* — bitter herbs, usually horseradish, which stand for the bitterness of slavery; *charoset* — a blend of fruits and nuts, to recall the bricks the Israelites made in the hot fields of Egypt; *zeroah* — a shank bone of a lamb, to represent the lamb that ancestors of the Jews ate in Egypt (vegetarians may use a broiled beet instead of a bone); and *betzah* — a roasted egg, a symbol of the new life the Israelites began after being slaves in Egypt.

At each plate on the seder table, there is a book called the *Haggadah*, from the Hebrew root meaning "to tell." During the seder, the people around the table read the story of Exodus, a retelling of how God freed the Israelites from slavery, and how Moses led them back to the Promised Land.

The story begins with the words "*Avadim hayinu*, We were slaves [in the land of Egypt]." This means that all Jews, not just their ancestors, were slaves to Pharaoh and were redeemed or saved. And, as people who were once slaves, they must not do to others what was once done to them.

Young people have two important jobs at the seder. First, the youngest child recites the Four Questions, beginning "*Mah nishtanah*, Why is this night different [from all other nights]?" which are answered by the person leading the seder. By questioning, children discover the story and meaning of Pesach, and prepare to play their part in continuing the three-thousand-year history of the Jewish people.

The second job for youngsters comes near the end of the seder. It is to look for the *afikomen*, a special wrapped piece of matzah that the leader hides at the start of the seder. The afikomen is the very last thing eaten at the end of the meal. Its taste is meant to stay in people's mouths for a long while. Hiding the afikomen has been said to refer to the Messiah, the Hidden One, who will bring about a time of peace and harmony for all. Someone pours a special cup of wine for the prophet Elijah and opens the door so that he may enter. According to tradition, Elijah will one day come to announce the Messiah.

The seder usually ends with songs and praise to God, without whom the Jewish people would still be slaves to Pharaoh in Egypt. The final words are often: "*L'shanah habah bi-Y'rushalayim*, Next year in Jerusalem." (Jerusalem means "City of Peace" in Hebrew.) It expresses the wish that next year all Jews will be at peace and one in spirit.

CRAFTS AND FOOD

MATZAH COVER • *All ages — with adult help.*
Three pieces of matzah are placed in separate slots of a matzah cover and set out for the seder meal.

YOU'LL NEED:

4 PIECES CLEAN, WHITE COTTON CLOTH, ABOUT

15 INCHES SQUARE

STRAIGHT PINS

FELT PEN

EMBROIDERY THREAD

NEEDLE AND THREAD

1. Make a pile of the 4 cloth pieces, and use straight pins to pin them together on all 4 sides.

2. Draw small, simple designs with the pen in each corner of the top cloth.

3. Embroider the 4 designs, bringing the needle and thread through all 4 pieces of cloth. (If you want, you can then sew together 3 sides of the matzah cover.)

4. Slip a piece of matzah into each of the 3 pockets of your matzah cover for the seder.

SEDER PLATE • *Ages 8 and up — with adult help.*

The seder plate is placed on the table in front of the leader.

YOU'LL NEED:

LARGE PLASTIC OR PAPER PLATE

FELT PEN

CLEAR, LIQUID PLASTIC SPRAY

DAMP SPONGE

1. Use felt pen to write the names of the 5 foods around edge of plate — karpas, maror, charoset, zeroah, and betzah.

2. Beneath each name, draw a circle in which you can later place the food.

3. Spray entire face of plate with clear, liquid plastic. Apply several light coats, waiting for each coat to dry before applying the next.

4. Repeat step 3 on back of plate.

5. Clean plate with a damp sponge.

6. Prepare the special foods and place them in the circles before the seder.

ASHKENAZIC CHAROSET • *Ages 8 and up — with adult help.*

YOU'LL NEED:

FOOD CHOPPER	2 APPLES, QUARTERED
MEDIUM-SIZED BOWL	AND CORED
MEASURING CUP	$\frac{1}{2}$ CUP CHOPPED WALNUTS
AND SPOONS	1 TEASPOON CINNAMON
WOODEN MIXING SPOON	2 TABLESPOONS GRAPE JUICE

1. Chop apples finely and place into bowl.

2. Add nuts and cinnamon.

3. Add grape juice. Stir until mixture sticks together.

Makes about 2 cups.

SEPHARDIC CHAROSET • *Ages 8 and up — with adult help.*

YOU'LL NEED:

FOOD CHOPPER

MEDIUM-SIZED BOWL

MEASURING CUP AND SPOONS

WOODEN MIXING SPOON

1 CUP FRESH DATES, WITH PITS REMOVED

$\frac{1}{2}$ CUP RAISINS

$\frac{1}{2}$ CUP CHOPPED WALNUTS

$\frac{1}{2}$ CUP CHOPPED ALMONDS

1 POMEGRANATE, QUARTERED

$\frac{1}{2}$ TEASPOON CINNAMON

$\frac{1}{4}$ TEASPOON GROUND GINGER

$\frac{1}{4}$ TEASPOON GROUND CLOVES

2 TABLESPOONS ORANGE JUICE

1. Chop dates and raisins and place into bowl.

2. Add nuts.

3. Scoop out pomegranate. Chop and add to mixture.

4. Add spices.

5. Add orange juice. Stir until mixture sticks together.

Makes about 2 cups.

MATZAH BALLS • *Ages 8 and up — with adult help.*

Chicken soup with matzah balls is the highpoint of any Pesach seder.

YOU'LL NEED:

SMALL MIXING BOWL	2 EGGS
WOODEN MIXING SPOON	2 TABLESPOONS CORN OIL
MEASURING CUP AND	2 TABLESPOONS WATER
SPOONS	$\frac{1}{2}$ CUP MATZAH MEAL
LARGE POT OF BOILING WATER	PINCH OF SALT
CHICKEN SOUP	PINCH OF PEPPER

1. Beat eggs lightly in mixing bowl.

2. Add other ingredients and mix.

3. Cover bowl and refrigerate for half an hour.

4. Form mixture into small balls and drop into large pot of boiling water.

5. Cover pot, lower to medium heat, and cook for half an hour.

6. Drain and serve in soup.

Makes 6 large matzah balls.

Shavuot

THE GIFT OF THE TORAH

"WHEN YOU COME INTO THE LAND WHICH I GIVE YOU . . .

YOU SHALL COUNT FROM THE DAY YOU HAVE BROUGHT THE FIRST FRUIT

SEVEN WEEKS . . . AND ON THE MORROW AFTER THE SEVENTH SABBATH

IT SHALL BE FIFTY DAYS, AND YOU SHALL PRESENT

A NEW MEAL OFFERING TO THE LORD."

Leviticus 23:10–16

THE ISRAELITES WERE FINALLY FREED from slavery. Moses had helped them escape from the land of Egypt and had led them on a long journey across the desert wilderness. Now, at last, they had arrived at the foot of Mount Sinai. It was the place where God had told Moses to bring the Children of Israel.

The people set up camp opposite the massive mountain. They put up their tents. They unpacked their few belongings.

God called Moses from the mountain. "Tell this to the Israelites: You have seen the plagues that I brought on the Egyptians. And you have seen how I have brought you here safely. Now, prepare yourselves to receive a great gift. It is called the Torah. It shall make you a great people."

God then added, "Tell the Israelites I am coming to you in a thick cloud. Thus may they hear God speaking to you and always believe you also."

Moses listened very carefully to God's words. Then Moses gathered together his people.

The great leader looked terribly solemn. "You saw how God freed us from slavery in Egypt," said Moses. "You saw how God opened the Red Sea to let us pass. You saw how God gave us *manna*, flakes of grain, and freshwater as we crossed the desert."

"Now," Moses went on, "God wishes to give us a most valuable and wonderful gift. It is a gift more precious that anything on Earth."

A woman cried out from the crowd, "What is it?"

"It is the Torah," Moses said. "In it are stories and laws to guide us and teach us how God wishes us to live. From the Torah, we can learn how to keep the peace with our neighbors. And we can learn how to live as a free people, not as slaves."

"Yes, yes!" the people shouted. "We shall do everything that God teaches us."

Moses continued, "God gladly gives you this gift. All that God asks is that you follow and obey the law. God will always be present to help and guide you."

"God's Torah is a great gift!" the people in the crowd cried again.

Moses was pleased. He told the people how to prepare themselves to receive the Torah. "Pray and purify yourselves for two days," he said. "On the morning of the third day be ready on the plain below the mountain."

For two days, the people washed their clothes and cleaned themselves. At dawn on the third day, they dressed carefully. Everyone assembled in the level clearing before Mount Sinai.

The Israelites huddled in small groups. Each person wondered what was going to happen.

They did not have long to wait. A heavy cloud came down and

swallowed them up in darkness. Blustering winds brought drenching rains. Lightning bolts hurtled down from the sky. The roar of thunder filled the air. Below their feet, the earth shook and quaked.

Out of the fearsome storm came a long, loud blast of a *shofar*, a ram's horn. The blare of the shofar grew louder and louder. Then, all at once, the sound stopped. A hush fell over everything.

The people fell back in awe as Moses went up alone on the mountain. As he neared the top, the people heard a mighty voice speak out of the cloud. God announced the Ten Commandments:

"I am the Lord your God, who brought you out of the land of Egypt.

"You shall have no other gods before me.

"You shall not take the name of God in vain.

"You shall remember the Sabbath day and keep it holy.

"Honor your father and your mother.

"You shall not kill.

"You shall not commit adultery.

"You shall not steal.

"You shall not bear false witness against your neighbor.

"You shall not covet anything that belongs to another."

The Israelites stood at the foot of Mount Sinai, dazed and frightened. They could not see Moses in the great black cloud at the top of the mountain. Uncertain what to do, the people returned to their dwellings.

Moses stayed with God for forty days and forty nights. During that time, Moses neither ate nor drank. God gave him many more laws and rules for the nation of Israel to follow.

As Moses was about to leave, God handed him two thin slabs, tablets of stone. On the stones were written the first Ten Commandments.

Meanwhile, the people below were growing restless. Day after day, they waited for Moses to come down from Mount Sinai. All in all, he was gone nearly seven weeks.

"Moses probably forgot us," many said. "Let us build a statue of a god that we can see. We can worship it. We can thank it for leading us out of Egypt."

So the people put together all their bits of gold. They melted rings, earrings, bracelets, and necklaces, and they formed an animal idol, a giant golden calf.

"Let us praise this calf, and honor it," the elders proclaimed.

God saw what was happening and grew angry.

"Why are you so cross?" Moses asked. "Have I wronged you?"

"No," God said, "but the people have. They have broken our Covenant. I promised to love and protect them. In exchange they promised to obey my laws. Now they're worshipping an idol!"

"An *idol*!" Moses exclaimed.

Moses was afraid that God would destroy the Children of Israel. So he begged God to forgive them.

Then Moses hurried down the mountain. In his hands, he held the Ten Commandments that God had inscribed on the two stone tablets.

The splendid man stopped on a rock just above the clearing. Below, the people were dancing and singing around the golden calf.

"Fools!" he thundered. "How could you be so quick to break your word to God?"

Moses raised high the tablets. Forcefully he hurled them down at the calf. The tablets shattered into pieces.

The huge crowd stood still in shocked silence.

Moses passed through. No one spoke or touched him. Ashamed of themselves, the Israelites watched as Moses sat down and wept.

Fear gripped the people on the next day. God's tablets lay broken on the ground. They wondered, What punishment would God send?

Moses spoke. "You have done wrong. You should be afraid. But God is forgiving."

Once more Moses went up on Mount Sinai. Again he asked God to forgive them. And God did.

Then God asked Moses to make two tablets like the ones he had smashed. God also gave Moses the design for a special box, called an ark, in which to keep the tablets.

"Write my Ten Commandments on these stones," God bade Moses. "And tell the people of my other rules. Explain that they must study all God's laws."

Moses left God and descended the mountain. He looked radiant. His face seemed to be giving off its own light. It streamed out in two beams from his silvery hair. Dressed in white, he stood very tall amid the flowers in the blooming desert.

Moses showed the people the new set of tablets. On them were engraved the laws God had just proclaimed.

"Will you obey these words of God?" he asked.

The elders came forward. They spoke for the people. "All that God has said we will do," they declared.

Then Moses said, "God has given an exact design for an ark to keep the tablets in. Everyone shall contribute to its making. It will be holy and perfect."

The people rushed to gather the many special materials God had ordered. Out of locust wood, goats' hair, gold, and onyx they crafted a magnificent ark. When it was finished, Moses placed the new tablets inside.

Soon it was time for Moses and his people to resume their journey to the Promised Land. They carried the ark from place to place. Within it were God's holy words. The words bound the Israelites into a nation.

Every place that they stopped, the people put the ark at the center of the camp. The first two commandments reminded them that they had one God who was ready to help them. The other commandments gave them simple laws to follow in order to live happily among all the peoples of the world.

In time, the people carried the Ten Commandments into the Promised Land. There they built the Temple, a House of God, in Jerusalem. Each Shavuot, when the first wheat and fruits were ripe, the people brought some of their crop to the holy Temple. This offering expressed their thanks to God for the Ten Commandments, for the Torah that guided them, and for the fruitful land that fed them.

The basic story was adapted from the Bible, Book of Exodus, Chapters 19, 20, 31, 32, and 34. The biblical account is read during synagogue services on the first day of Shavuot.

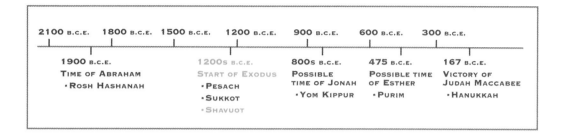

WHAT WE CELEBRATE

THE FESTIVAL OF SHAVUOT, which means "weeks" in Hebrew, originally celebrated the cutting of the spring wheat. Later, it also came to mark the giving of the Ten Commandments to Moses on Mount Sinai. Judaism believes that God gave 613 commandments in the Torah, which is the first five books of the Bible. Of these, the Ten Commandments are an essential part. They give people ideas of justice, kindness, and peace by which to live.

The festival of Shavuot is also called the Feast of Weeks. That is because it comes seven weeks, or a week of weeks, seven times seven, after the first day of Pesach. Shavuot falls on the sixth and seventh days of Sivan, which usually begins sometime in late May or early June. In addition, the holiday completes the story of the Exodus. At Pesach the Israelites were freed from slavery. At Shavuot they became a nation, having received the law from God.

The Bible denotes Shavuot as *Hag hakatzir*, "Festival of the Harvest," and also *Yom habikkurim*, "Day of First Fruits." According to tradition, the Hebrews brought a thanksgiving offering of two loaves of bread, "the first fruits of wheat harvest," to the Temple in Jerusalem on this day. The two loaves represent the two tablets of the Ten Commandments and were the traditional offering to God in the early years of Jewish history.

How We Celebrate

SHAVUOT IS A GAY AND JOYOUS HOLIDAY. People decorate their homes and synagogues with greens and fresh flowers. One explanation is that Mount Sinai, a dry, desert mountain, burst into bloom on the day that the Ten Commandments were revealed to Moses. Another says the custom recalls the bringing of the first fruits to the Temple in Jerusalem.

In the synagogue, the reading of the Ten Commandments is a very important part of the Shavuot service. During the reading, the congregation stands as the ancients once stood at Sinai.

Since Shavuot marks the Covenant with God, parents often start the education of their children at this time of year. Young Jewish adults, who have already become *bar* or *bat mitzvah*, are confirmed on this holiday. The confirmation ceremony reaffirms their commitment to Judaism and the Jewish people.

Many people celebrate Shavuot by staying awake all night studying the Torah. According to legend some Israelites overslept on the day God gave them the Ten Commandments and had to be awakened by Moses. Thus, going without sleep and studying Torah shows an eagerness to receive the law.

People also read the Book of Ruth on the second day of Shavuot. The story tells how Ruth, a non-Jew from Moab, marries a Jew from Judah and later converts, freely accepting the Jewish faith. Thus, Ruth embraced Judaism, just as the Israelites accepted the Torah. Many of the Shavuot celebrations are also connected to the spring harvest.

Milk and dairy dishes, especially cheesecake and *blintzes*, folded pancakes filled with cheese, are eaten on Shavuot. Some say that the people were too tired and hungry to cook after their long wait to receive the Torah. So they rushed back to their tents and ate milk and cheese and other easy-to-prepare foods. Others claim the tradition comes from the sentence in the Bible, "And God gave us this land, a land flowing with milk and honey."

CRAFTS AND FOOD

STAINED-GLASS FLOWER PICTURE • *All ages — with adult help.*

You can tape your stained-glass flower picture to a window. This follows the old custom of placing paper flowers on windows for Shavuot.

YOU'LL NEED:

FLOWERS, SOME FLOWER PETALS, OR SOME LEAVES

WAXED PAPER

NEWSPAPER

STEAM IRON

SCISSORS

PASTE

CONSTRUCTION PAPER

1. Place flowers, flower petals, or leaves between 2 pieces of waxed paper.

2. Cover waxed paper with newspaper and have an adult help you gently press all over with a warm steam iron. (The heat will melt the waxed paper, sealing the flower, the petals, or the leaves inside.)

3. Carefully trim the waxed paper with scissors, and paste strips of construction paper around the edges to make a frame.

4. Tape or hang in a window facing the street.

SHAVUOT FAMILY TREE • *All ages.*

It is a beautiful Shavuot tradition to decorate the home with flowers, leaves, and boughs of trees. A family tree can celebrate the giving of the Torah, as it reminds Jews of their place in the tradition of their ancestors.

YOU'LL NEED:

LARGE TREE BRANCH WITH SMALLER BRANCHES COMING OFF MAIN BRANCH

5-INCH BY 8-INCH INDEX CARDS OR PIECES OF THIN CARDBOARD

FELT PEN

GREEN CRAYON

SCISSORS

GLUE, PINS, OR STAPLER

BUCKET OR WASTEBASKET

SAND OR PEBBLES

1. Trace 1 of your hands for each family member on an index card or piece of cardboard. (Include grandparents, uncles and aunts, and cousins, as well as your immediate family.)
2. Write each person's name inside a hand. Color cards green.
3. Carefully cut out hand shape, and glue, pin, or staple the card to the end of a branch.
4. Fill bucket or wastebasket with sand or pebbles and stand your family tree inside.

CHEESE BLINTZES • *Ages 8 and up — with adult help.*

In keeping with the custom of eating dairy foods on Shavuot, here's a recipe that you're sure to love.

YOU'LL NEED:

2 SMALL MIXING BOWLS

1 MEDIUM MIXING BOWL

EGG BEATER

MEASURING CUP AND SPOONS

NONSTICK FRYING PAN

WAXED PAPER

FILLING

YOU'LL NEED:

1 POUND COTTAGE CHEESE

1 EGG YOLK

$^1/_2$ TEASPOON SALT

1 TABLESPOON SUGAR

1. Mix all filling ingredients thoroughly in a small bowl.

2. Place bowl in refrigerator for 1 hour.

3. Do this before making blintzes.

BLINTZES

YOU'LL NEED:

$^3/_4$ CUP FLOUR

1 CUP ICE WATER

2 EGGS

$^1/_4$ TEASPOON SALT

2 TABLESPOONS MELTED BUTTER

OIL FOR FRYING

1. Stir flour and water in medium mixing bowl until smooth.

2. Beat eggs with salt in a small mixing bowl. Add to flour and water.

3. Add melted butter to flour mixture. Stir until smooth.

4. Heat frying pan.

5. Drop in only enough batter to form a thin layer that completely covers the bottom of the frying pan. (Tip pan to spread batter around evenly.)

6. Fry 1 side only until batter gets dry around edges.

7. Remove from pan and place on waxed paper, fried side up.

8. Repeat steps 5, 6, and 7 until all batter is used up.

9. Place a heaping tablespoon of filling along bottom edge. Fold in right and left sides and then roll up from the bottom.

10. Fry in a little oil on both sides until brown and crispy. Serve with sour cream.

Makes 12 blintzes.

Index